Design
Agendas

1   Aerial view of the St. Louis riverfront, 1933.

Design Agendas:

Modern Architecture in St. Louis, 1930s–1970s

Edited by
Eric P. Mumford

With contributions by
Shantel Blakely
John C. Guenther
Kathleen James-Chakraborty
Eric P. Mumford
Winifred Elysse Newman
Michael E. Willis

Mildred Lane Kemper Art Museum
Sam Fox School of Design & Visual Arts
Washington University in St. Louis

This volume is published on occasion of the exhibition
Design Agendas: Modern Architecture in St. Louis, 1930s–1970s,
on view at the Kemper Art Museum from September 13, 2024,
to January 6, 2025.

Mildred Lane Kemper Art Museum
Sam Fox School of Design & Visual Arts
Washington University in St. Louis
MSC 1214-203-208
St. Louis, Missouri 63130
kemperartmuseum.wustl.edu

This publication was made possible by the support
of the William T. Kemper Foundation.

Editor
Eric P. Mumford

Editorial liaison
Sabine Eckmann

Managing editor
Jane E. Neidhardt

Contributing editor
Holly Tasker

Research assistants
Mary Reid Brunstrom, Kristin Good,
Leslie Markle, Holly Tasker

Indexer
Flatpage

Designer
Lorraine Wild and Naveen Hattis,
Green Dragon Office, Los Angeles

Printer
Pristone, Singapore

Typeset in ABC Marfa by Dinamo
and Doppel-Mittel Egyptienne
by Forgotten Shapes

Distributed by
The University of Chicago Press
11030 S. Langley Avenue
Chicago, Illinois 60628
press.uchicago.edu

Domestic
1-800-621-2736
Fax: 1-800-621-8476

International
1-773-702-7000
Fax: 1-773-702-7212

Library of Congress Control Number
2024935475

ISBN
978-0-936316-50-5

Printed and bound in Singapore

Mildred Lane
Kemper Art Museum

Washington University in St. Louis
SAM FOX SCHOOL OF DESIGN & VISUAL ARTS

Contents

2   Aerial view of the St. Louis riverfront after demolition for the Jefferson National Expansion Memorial (Gateway Arch), c. 1942.

Foreword

This reader, which was published to accompany the exhibition *Design Agendas: Modern Architecture in St. Louis, 1930s–1970s*, examines modern architecture and its discontents, taking St. Louis as a case study. The modern movement in architecture began to appear in St. Louis in the mid-1930s, coinciding with the growing interest for modern, frequently European, art by art institutions and private collectors such as Joseph Pulitzer Jr. and Morton D. May, among others. The modern structures built in this city during this period and into the 1970s encompass a wide array of building types: private houses, medical facilities, public monuments, churches, and commercial structures. The architects involved include national figures (Charles E. Fleming, Gyo Obata, Eero Saarinen, Minoru Yamasaki), local and regional practitioners (Harris Armstrong, Eugene J. Mackey Jr., Joseph D. Murphy) and such lesser-known figures as Albert Osburg.

This reader studies the various manifestations of St. Louis modern(ist) architecture, including hybrid buildings that combine the historicist with the modern in often unexpected and eclectic ways, as in the Homer G. Phillips Hospital by Osburg. Is also addresses the often-complex alignments between modernist aesthetic aspirations and the programmatic as well as pragmatic requirements of certain building types; this can be seen in many of the structures designed by Fleming and is also evident in the Lambert–St. Louis Airport terminal (Hellmuth, Yamasaki + Leinweber). Perhaps most importantly, this reader argues for a parallel modernism, one that did not compete with the canonical rational and functional International Style as promoted by the Museum of Modern Art and the director of its architecture department, Philip Johnson. It found its own voice straddling the visually spectacular and aestheticizing— as realized, for example, in Saarinen's Jefferson National Expansion Memorial (Gateway Arch) and Obata's Priory Chapel (Abbey Church of Saint Louis Priory School)—embracing the unembellished language of modernism through advanced technologies.

The legacies of modernism in architecture, not unlike those in the visual arts, are complex rather than dichotomous or straightforward. At different moments during the twentieth century, they intersected—locally, nationally, and internationally—with various other developments and agendas in urban planning, architecture, and politics. As much as modernism tried to advance democratic ideals of social justice—a case in point being the Bauhaus— so too did it reveal its inevitable malleability when it came to melding aesthetic form with the politics of nationalism and expansionism. This is witnessed, for example, in the Gateway Arch, which commemorates Thomas Jefferson and US westward expansion to celebrate the country, region, and city as powerful shapers of a global future.

Coinciding with the appearance of modern architecture in St. Louis, however, was the region's and city's willingness to demolish historical sites that would have served as important documents of the vagaries of colonial settlement. All the same, modernism in architecture and the visual arts had strong inclinations to do away with the past, even attack it, especially the legacy of classical antiquity and its varied revivals. These erasures were to make place not necessarily for certain urgent needs of the present but for what is often described as a utopian future. As so-called efforts of slum area clearances, these eradications particularly affected African American communities and other marginalized groups in this city. The essays in this volume are the first to critically contextualize the history of modern architecture in St. Louis from the 1930s to the advent of postmodernism within this context of displacement and segregation.

Although the Kemper Art Museum does not hold a collection of design- or architecture-related materials, it has a more-than-decade-long history of presenting architecture and design in critical exhibitions. Examples include *Birth of the Cool* (2008–9), *Eero Saarinen: Shaping the Future* (2009), *Metabolic City* (2009–10), *Design with the Other 90%: Cities* (2012–13), *On the Thresholds of Space-Making: Shinohara Kazuo and His Legacy* (2014), *Drawing Ambience: Alvin Boyarsky and the Architectural Association* (2014–15), and *Transformative Visions: Washington University's East End, Then and Now* (2018). Many of these projects illuminated a broad spectrum of modern and contemporary architectural practices and oeuvres, including visionary proposals—both utopian and dystopian—architects' drawings, and monographs devoted to Saarinen and Shinohara. Many were curated by members of the faculty of the College and Graduate School of Architecture, part of Washington University's Sam Fox School of Design & Visual Arts. Continuing this tradition, *Design Agendas* is curated by Eric P. Mumford, the Rebecca and John Voyles Professor of Architecture, and Michael E. Willis, visiting faculty, distinguished architect, and alumnus. My congratulations to both of them for their committed and enthusiastic work on both the exhibition and this publication. Their success has resulted in a critical interrogation and revision of the complex history of modern architecture and city planning while providing glimpses into how the development of the built environment might enable St. Louis to overcome past social injustices.

Design Agendas: Modern Architecture in St. Louis, 1930s–1970s would not have been possible without the support of members of the Director's Circle, Emily and Teddy Greenspan, Michael Forman and Jennifer Rice, Julie Kemper Foyer, Joanne Gold and Andrew Stern, David and Dorothy Kemper, Ron and Pamela Mass, and Kim and Bruce Olson, the Hortense Lewin Art Fund, the Ken and Nancy Kranzberg Fund, and members of the Mildred Lane Kemper Art Museum. Without this generous support we would not be able to delve deep into significant histories such as here. Profound appreciation goes to Carmon Colangelo, the Ralph J. Nagel Dean of the Sam Fox School of Design & Visual Arts, for his commitment to the Museum and its programs, and to Provost and Executive Vice Chancellor Beverly Wendland and Chancellor Andrew Martin for continuing the University's priority of supporting the arts on campus.

Sabine Eckmann
William T. Kemper Director
and Chief Curator
Mildred Lane Kemper Art Museum

Contributors

Shantel Blakely is Assistant Professor of Architecture at Rice University.

John C. Guenther, FAIA, LEED AP, is the founder and principal of John C. Guenther Architect LLC.

Kathleen James-Chakraborty is Professor of Art History at University College Dublin.

Eric P. Mumford is the Rebecca and John Voyles Professor of Architecture in the Sam Fox School of Design & Visual Arts at Washington University in St. Louis.

Winifred Elysse Newman is the Homer Curtis Mickel and Leola Carter Mickel Professor of Architecture; Associate Dean for Research and Faculty Affairs; and Director of the Institute for Intelligent Materials, Systems and Environments (CU-iMSE) in the School of Architecture and College of Architecture, Art and Construction at Clemson University.

Michael E. Willis, FAIA, NOMA, is a design consultant and the founder and retired principal of MWA Architects.

Page 12
3   Eero Saarinen's Jefferson National Expansion Memorial (Gateway Arch) under construction, St. Louis, 1965.

Acknowledgments

This book and the related exhibition were made possible by the support and encouragement of Sabine Eckmann, William T. Kemper Director and Chief Curator at the Mildred Lane Kemper Art Museum, and Carmon Colangelo, Ralph J. Nagel Dean and E. Desmond Lee Professor for Collaboration in the Arts, both at the Sam Fox School of Design & Visual Arts at Washington University in St. Louis. I am grateful to them for their continuing commitment to this effort.

At the Kemper Art Museum, the work of Jane Neidhardt, head of publications, and Holly Tasker, production editor; Kristin Good, associate registrar; Mark Ryan, assistant director for collections and exhibitions; and Leslie Markle, curator for public art, have been essential to the success of this project. At earlier stages Mary Reid Brunstrom provided important research assistance. I am also grateful to Naveen Hattis and Lorraine Wild at Green Dragon Office for their exceptional design for this book.

Many archivists helped identify, find, and in some cases reproduce the documents and photographs included here. My gratitude to Sonya Rooney and Miranda Rechtenwald at Washington University Libraries' Julian Edison Department of Special Collections; Rina Vecchiola, Jenny Akins, and James Gardner at the University's Kenneth and Nancy Kranzberg Art & Architecture Library; Jennifer Clark at the Gateway Arch National Park Archives; and many others, including at the Missouri Historical Society, the St. Louis Mercantile Library at the University of Missouri–St Louis, the Missouri Botanical Garden, the Chicago History Museum, the Cranbrook Archives, the Archives of Michigan, and the Erich Mendelsohn Archive, Staatliche Museen, Berlin.

For their loans of material and enthusiasm for this publication and its companion exhibition, I thank Dennis Cope; Kathryn Feldt and Lydia Nunes at the Frank Lloyd Wright House in Ebsworth Park; Lucy Gossett at the Center of Contemporary Arts; Chris Grubbs; John C. Guenther; Bob Hansman; Patty Heyda; John Hoal; Bruce Lindsey; Kiku Obata; Emily Pulitzer; Brother Sixtus Roslevich, formerly at the Saint Louis Abbey School; Carl Safe; Peter Shank; and the St. Ann Catholic Church. Thanks also to Larissa Sattler for making the digital maps used in the exhibition.

For sharing their knowledge about these topics with me at various points over the past decades, I would like to convey my deep appreciation to Mark Abbott, Michael R. Allen, Matt Bernstine, Susan Bower, Wyly Brown, Iain Fraser, Catalina Freixas, Esley Hamilton, Jim Harris, Joseph Heathcott, Derek Hoeferlin, Kathleen James-Chakraborty, Sung Ho Kim, Jim Kohn, Stephen Leet, Gay Lorberbaum, Robert McCarter, Mariana Melin-Corcoran, Robert J. Moore Jr., Kelley Van Dyck Murphy, Winifred Elysse Newman, Andrew Raimist, Linda Samuels, Eric Sandweiss, Jessica Senne, Steve Skrairka, Geoff Ward, Cynthia Weese, Ted Wight, and Heather Woofter.

Foremost I want to express my deep appreciation to Michael E. Willis and the contributing authors for applying their expertise to advance our understanding of St. Louis's important spatial and architectural developments within their midcentury context. Last but far from least I offer my heartfelt thanks to Charles E. Fleming for his willingness to share his archives and his important historical accounts of previously little-known aspects of the topic.

Eric P. Mumford
Rebecca and John Voyles Professor of Architecture
Sam Fox School of Design & Visual Arts

Introduction

Eric P. Mumford

Design Agendas: Modern Architecture in St. Louis, 1930s–1970s
is the first major examination of the complex connections
in St. Louis between modern architecture, urban renewal, and
racial and spatial change in the interlocking histories of New
Deal planning, the Great Migration, and the Civil Rights and Great
Society eras. Offering insight into the ideological aims and
contextual conditions of the built environment in midcentury
St. Louis, the essays in this book also include close studies of the
regional work of Charles E. Fleming, Buckminster Fuller, Eric
Mendelsohn, and Gyo Obata as well as a personal reflection
by the architect Michael E. Willis, FAIA, NOMA, about the origins
of his career and his roots growing up in some of the buildings
and neighborhoods explored in this volume.

Many of the architectural works discussed here were created
in a period of de facto racial segregation, an era that is now known
for its often racist and destructive modernist urban planning,
such as the Pruitt-Igoe public housing project (1950–56) and the
clearance of the Mill Creek Valley neighborhood with the forced
displacement of its 20,000 Black residents (1959).[1] These and
other urban renewal initiatives at this time were also part
of several interrelated design agendas that used modern architecture and planning to propose and express new and then
thought to be more liberating ideas about social organization
and new forms of architecture and planning.

These efforts also resulted in new forms of architecture for the general public, including not only Eero Saarinen's Gateway Arch (1947–65) on the riverfront in downtown St. Louis, which was cleared in 1939–42 (figs. 1–3), but also many other highly visible public works. These include Mendelsohn's former B'nai Amoona Synagogue (1946–50); large slum-clearance public housing projects such as Pruitt-Igoe by Minoru Yamasaki with the firm of Hellmuth, Yamasaki + Leinweber (1950–56) as well as his Lambert-St. Louis Airport terminal; Obata's Priory Chapel (1956–62), along with other early works by HOK, the firm that he co-founded in 1956; various projects in the 1960s and 1970s by Fleming, one of the few Black architects working in St. Louis in this period; and Fuller's unbuilt visionary megastructural project for East St. Louis, Old Man River's City (1970–73). The expressive and innovative technologies used in these structures also indicated that a new era had begun in St. Louis, related to international trends of the time.

My essay here addresses some of the larger historical patterns around the appearance of modern architecture in a period of massive urban and spatial transformations.[2] Kathleen James-Chakraborty, a leading scholar of the work of Eric Mendelsohn, situates his former B'nai Amoona synagogue in the context of changing social and demographic circumstances and discusses how it offered a new model of religious buildings as suburban community centers. Winifred Elysse Newman, a former architectural design associate of Gyo Obata's, provides an account of his early work. Obata was a 1945 graduate of the Washington University School of Architecture who had narrowly escaped internment as a Japanese-American in the San Francisco Bay area during World War II. He went on to design several major works in and around St. Louis and to successfully negotiate the then-segregated and changing social landscape of this region; HOK eventually became the world's largest architecture firm. John C. Guenther, FAIA, LEED AP, a St. Louis practicing architect with extensive knowledge of modern architectural history, offers the first in-depth account of Buckminster Fuller's Old Man River's City, proposed for the newly Black-majority city of East St. Louis at the request of the Black dance pioneer and arts patron Katherine Dunham. The architectural historian Shantel Blakely provides the first account of the career of Charles E. Fleming, the first Black graduate in Architecture at Washington University (University College, 1961) in the Civil Rights era.

Technological innovation in architecture was a key aspect
of the work of this period, from the thin-shell concrete construction used at Lambert Airport and Priory Chapel,
to the geodesic dome concept of Fuller that was used by other
architects at the Missouri Botanical Garden Climatron (1960)
in his other local works. There are also many other modern
religious buildings, public schools, campuses, and commercial
facilities that were designed here in related ways as well.
Although sometimes threatened with demolition, many of these
works are still appreciated and continue to be important
elements of the metropolitan life of the St. Louis region.

The early modern projects in St. Louis were in various ways
identified as "modern" in the 1930s, and some of these were
published nationally in architectural magazines. At the time, the
term modern was also used to describe such different design

5   Isamu Noguchi, ceiling of the American Stove Company building (later Magic Chef), St. Louis, 1946–47, colorized photograph c. 1948.

6   Harris Armstrong, American Stove Company building (later Magic Chef), St. Louis, 1946–47, elevation from South Kingshighway.

directions as what is now often termed Art Deco, Streamline Moderne, or Stripped Classicism. For what is now usually called "midcentury modern" in architecture, the impact of the 1932 Museum of Modern Art exhibition *Modern Architecture: International Exhibition*[3] was extensive across the country, as were the contemporaneous though different approaches of Frank Lloyd Wright, Eric Mendelsohn, and Eliel Saarinen.[4] The International Style, a version of European functionalism defined mostly by its formal rather than its social characteristics, such as flat roofs, white walls, and horizontal strip windows, is visible in Harris Armstrong's Shanley building, a small dental clinic in Clayton, a suburb of St. Louis (1935; fig. 4).[5] In the 1940s Armstrong became one of the leading modern architects in St. Louis and an inspiration to many younger ones, including Fleming and Michael E. Willis.[6] He also commissioned the Japanese-American sculptor Isamu Noguchi to design the molded plaster ceiling at the American Stove Company headquarters (1946–47, figs. 5, 6; altered). The impact of the International Style can also be seen in the Morton D. May House in Ladue (1941; demolished) by the Chicago architect Samuel Marx (fig. 7).

7 Samuel Marx, Morton D. May residence,
Ladue, Missouri, 1941, photograph 1942.

Around the same time a different kind of modern work, what
would now be described as Art Deco, was also being built;
this is visible in some of the ornamentation in the original Homer
G. Phillips Hospital (1937; fig. 8), which was designed as a segregated facility by the city architect Albert Osburg for what
was then one of the city's few Black neighborhoods, the Ville.
Unusually for such a project, it introduced some of the world's
most advanced technical aspects of a modern hospital at the
time, including its Y-shaped form with multiple elevators
and spaces for air handling and new technical equipment within
an eclectically styled brick exterior.[7]

Other modern houses and small business and medical buildings
soon followed, some influenced by the teaching and practice
of Eliel Saarinen at the Cranbrook Academy of Art, which the distinguished Finnish architect had founded near Detroit in 1924. These
included the Meyer House (1936–38; fig. 9) by Charles Eames

and Robert Walsh, designed before Eames attended Cranbrook and moved in a more modern design direction with Ray Kaiser; both were students of Saarinen's son Eero Saarinen at Cranbrook.[8] Other public examples of this "Cranbrook moment" of architecture in St. Louis include Armstrong's Grant Medical Clinic (1938; fig. 10), Eames's stone base for the sculpture *Meeting of the Waters* (1939) in front of Union Station by the Cranbrook-trained artist Carl Milles, and Joseph D. Murphy and Kenneth Wischmeyer's Municipal Opera (1939; the Muny) in Forest Park. These works appeared at the same time as what was described as the first modern church in St. Louis, St. Mark's Episcopal Church (1939) in the St. Louis Hills area of the city, designed by Charles Nagel Jr. and Frederick Wallace Dunn.[9]

8   Albert Osburg, Homer G. Phillips Hospital, St. Louis, 1937, postcard c. 1940.

After the war, the MIT-educated Joseph Murphy began a series of major commissions for the Catholic Church under the leadership of Archbishop Joseph Ritter, who began to desegregate church institutions and parochial schools at this time. This was a controversial decision among the Catholic community, yet it sparked a nationwide trend in doing so.[10] An admirer of Mendelsohn's work, Murphy included in his St. Ann Catholic Church (1947–51; fig. 11) design elements found at the time in the work of both Eliel Saarinen and Mendelsohn, including

9   Eames & Walsh, John and Alice Meyer residence, Huntleigh, Missouri, 1937.

10   Harris Armstrong, Grant Medical Clinic, St. Louis, 1938, altered.

11   Joseph D. Murphy, St. Ann Catholic Church,
Normandy, Missouri, 1947–51, model 1947.

12 Eliel Saarinen, First Christian Church, Columbus,
Indiana, 1940–42, rendering by Charles Eames c. 1939.

Pages 24–25
13 Joseph D. Murphy, St. Ann Catholic Church,
Normandy, Missouri, 1947–51, sanctuary interior,
stained glass window by Emil Frei studio.

smooth, mostly unornamented exterior and interior surfaces
whose characteristics changed in different kinds of light.
With this project he created a new kind of suburban church,
boldly visible amid new strip development along Natural Bridge
Road, then a major corridor of suburban development.

St. Ann's interior had column-free sightlines, somewhat like Eliel
Saarinen's First Christian Church in Columbus, Indiana (1940–42;
fig. 12), and it focused on an immense stained glass window
by Robert Harmon of the Emil Frei studio (fig. 13), one of many
that Harmon would design for churches in the region.[11] These
included Murphy and Mackey's Resurrection Church (1954; fig. 14)
in the Dutchtown neighborhood of the city, and many others,
mostly in the suburbs.[12] Their churches and other works such
as Bishop DuBourg High School (1949; fig. 15) were also opportunities for them to apply to sacred architecture the modernist
principles that Murphy was instrumental in establishing as the
first dean of the School of Architecture at Washington
University. This formalized the School's then a ready emerging
shift away from a prewar Beaux-Arts pedagogy.[13]

After 1945 modern architecture thus began to become mainstream in St. Louis, though not without controversy, as many
residential areas retained their traditional designs. Major local
examples of modern works include the Russell and Ruth Kraus
House by Frank Lloyd Wright (1951–55; figs. 16, 17).[14] Houses
by Harris Armstrong, William Adair Bernoudy, Charles and Doris
Danna, Robert Elkington, Murphy and Mackey Isadore Shank,
and others—most still privately owned—also demonstrated this
new direction, including Elkington's own residence (the Glass
House; fig. 18). Entire subdivisions of middle-class modern
houses were also designed by architects, such as Ralph and
Mary Jane Fournier's Ridgewood neighborhood in nearby
Crestwood (1950).[15]

In 1934 Bernoudy enrolled as a yearlong Taliesin Fellow to live,
study, and work with Wright as part of latter's Taliesin architectural apprenticeship program in Wisconsin in 1934 and 1935.[16]
On his return to St. Louis he began to design a series of houses
that applied Wright's design principles, some in partnership with
Edouard Mutrux, who also sometimes designed in the
Streamline Moderne mode (see for example Samuel A. Bassett's
medical office and residence; fig. 19). These Wright-inspired
projects included a spacious pool house for Joseph Pulitzer Jr.,

14   Murphy and Mackey, Resurrection of Our Lord
Church, St. Louis, 1954.

15   Murphy and Mackey, Bishop DuBourg High School,
St. Louis, 1949, rendering.

16 Frank Lloyd Wright, Russell and Ruth Kraus residence, Kirkwood, Missouri, 1951–55, living and dining areas.

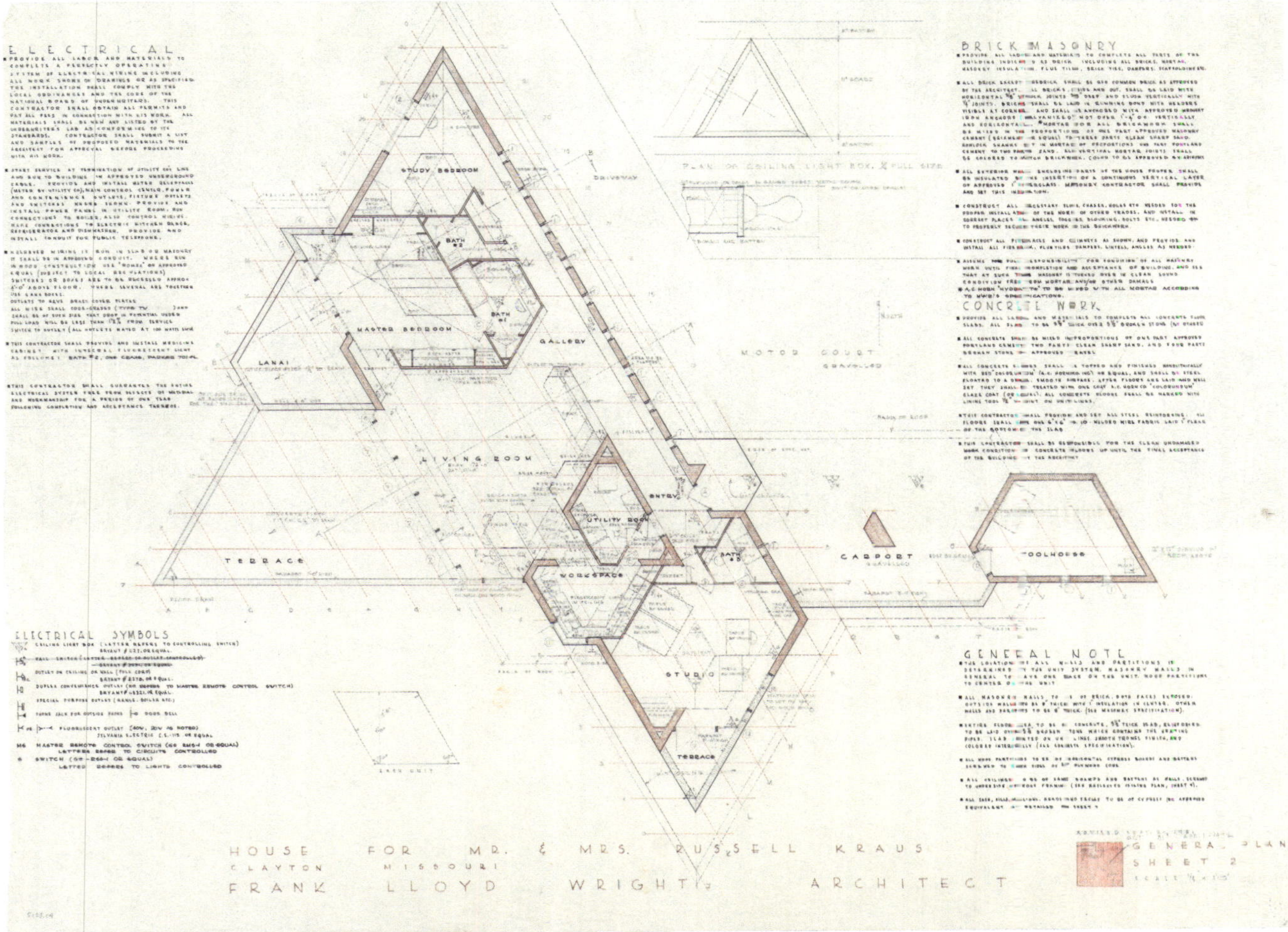

17 Frank Lloyd Wright, Russell and Ruth Kraus residence, Kirkwood, Missouri, 1951–55, plan.

18   Robert Elkington, Elkington residence,
Ballwin, Missouri, 1948.

19   Edouard Jules Mutrux / U. T. Taylor and Company, Samuel A. Bassett medical office and residence, Richmond Heights, Missouri, 1938, exterior modified with grey paint.

20 William Adair Bernoudy, Joseph Pulitzer Jr. pavilion and pool, Ladue, Missouri, 1948, with Jacques Lipchitz, *Figure* (1926–30), now in the collection of the Saint Louis Art Museum.

21   William Adair Bernoudy, Joseph Pulitzer Jr. pavilion,
Ladue, Missouri, 1948.

where Pulitzer displayed his growing collection of modern art, much of it now in the Harvard Art Museums (1948; figs. 20, 21).[17] Bernoudy's work also sometimes reflected his more literal use of some elements of Japanese domestic architecture, such as wood screens, garden and water elements, and raised outdoor terraces with lanterns.

In school construction, the first modern schools in St. Louis appeared post–World War II, notably the Toussaint L'Ouverture School by Charles Lorenz and Kenneth Wischmeyer (1948; fig. 22), which was the first modern school for Black students in the then still segregated St. Louis City public school system. An architecturally better-known example was the Swiss architect Alfred Roth's Holy Ghost Catholic Church and School in the all-white suburb of Berkeley in North County (1950; fig. 23), where Lorenz also designed the new high school (demolished).[18] Roth designed his building with Hellmuth, Yamasaki + Leinweber, who were then doing related educational work in the Detroit area. College campuses also began to use modern architecture in the 1950s, following Ludwig Mies van der Rohe's new Illinois Institute of Technology (IIT) campus in Chicago (1945–58).

22 Lorenz & Wischmeyer, L'Ouverture School, St. Louis, 1948.

23   Alfred Roth, former Holy Ghost Roman Catholic
Church and School, Berkeley, Missouri, 1950.

At Washington University, Harris Armstrong designed a new laboratory building for the Medical School in 1948, even as the University was still constructing modernized Gothic buildings on what is now the Danforth Campus. This was followed by the Olin Library competition in 1955, where the invited entrants included Louis I. Kahn, though the winning scheme was by Murphy and Mackey (1956; altered).

The influence of the Harvard Graduate School of Design (GSD)—created in 1936 by Harvard University President James B. Conant and Dean Joseph Hudnut, and led from 1937 to 1951 by Walter Gropius, the German émigré founder and first director of the Bauhaus (1919–28)—also began to impact the region in the 1950s. In 1955 Fumihiko Maki, a recent GSD graduate and former student of Josep Lluís Sert, who served as dean at Harvard from 1953 to 1969, arrived to teach at Washington University's School of Architecture. One of Murphy's successors as dean, Joseph Passonneau, a former Gropius GSD student, helped Maki with the structural design of his first commission, Mark C. Steinberg Hall on the University's Danforth Campus (1960; fig. 24). Passonneau also continued to invite Buckminster Fuller to campus to offer three-week courses in which students built geodesic domes from various materials,[19] a direction that

     INTRODUCTION

24   Fumihiko Maki, Mark C. Steinberg Hall,
Washington University, St. Louis, 1960, photograph 1983.

25   Murphy and Mackey with Synergetics Inc.,
Missouri Botanical Garden Climatron, St. Louis, 1960.

culminated at the Missouri Botanical Garden Climatron (1960; fig. 25), for which Murphy and Mackey served as the architects of record, with the Fuller-founded firm of Synergetics Inc. as the engineers.[20] Passonneau also invited members of the mostly European Team 10 group to teach as design studio visiting critics, notably Jacob Bakema in the 1959–60 academic year and Aldo van Eyck in 1961–62, both from the Netherlands.[21]

These various midcentury currents of modern architecture— the influence of Eliel Saarinen at Cranbrook, the teaching and example of Frank Lloyd Wright at Taliesin, the national impact of the International Style advanced by the Museum of Modern Art, and the pedagogical model of Gropius's Harvard GSD with its mostly unpublicized links to CIAM (International Congresses of Modern Architecture)—all combined in a still racially segregated environment to produce what is now called modern architecture in St. Louis. These directions were also often then seen as part of the more pragmatic, Robert Moses–type modernism of American slum clearance public housing, which was being carried out in St. Louis as well as in other major cities at this time.[22]

By the late 1960s, as the destructive impacts of urban clearance and the segregating aspects of modernism began to become clear, some new design directions were attempted to create a more racially integrated region.[23] LaClede Town (1963), one of most important of these experiments, was relatively successful until the 1980s as a mixed-use, low-rise, high-density, diverse community.[24] Starting in the 1970s, however, much of the focus in the city, though not in the surrounding region, shifted to the historic preservation of urban neighborhoods, with the idea that white flight could be halted or even reversed by investing in urban communities, including improving and extending mass transit, social services, and small-scale businesses to serve local residents and provide job opportunities. It was in this same context that Charles E. Fleming was commissioned to design many social service buildings, including the St. Louis Comprehensive Neighborhood Health Center (1974; fig. 26), and to renovate numerous parks across the city.[25]

These preservation efforts emerged after the evident failures of modern slum clearance and public housing, notorious after the nationally televised test demolition of the first buildings of Pruitt-Igoe in 1972; reuse and preservation in St. Louis continue to be advocated for, sometimes successfully, up to the present day.

26   Jenkins-Fleming Inc., St. Louis Comprehensive
Neighborhood Health Center, 1974.

1   For a first-person account of life in Mill Creek Valley, see Vivian Gibson, *The Last Children of Mill Creek* (Cleveland: Belt, 2020); for an urban history of the area, see Ron Fagerstrom, *Mill Creek Valley: A Soul of St. Louis* (St. Louis, 2010).

2   For an overview of the emergence of modern architecture in the region as it related to the School of Architecture at Washington University, see Eric Mumford, ed., *Modern Architecture in St. Louis: Washington University and Postwar American Architecture, 1948–1973* (St. Louis: Belt, 2004). For examples of the variety of design directions then called "modern," see David Conradsen and Genevieve Cortinovis, *St. Louis Modern* (St. Louis; Saint Louis Art Museum, 2015).

3   The exhibition *Modern Architecture: International Exhibition* was accompanied by the publication *The International Style: Architecture since 1922*, by Henry-Russell Hitchcock Jr. and Philip Johnson (New York: Museum of Modern Art, 1932).

4   On Eliel Saarinen and Cranbrook, see David G. De Long, "Eliel Saarinen and the Cranbrook Tradition in Architecture and Urban Design," in Robert Judson Clark, et al., *Design in America: The Cranbrook Vision* (New York: Abrams, 1983), 46–89.

5   Andrew Raimist, "Harris Armstrong's Shanley Building, 1935," *Society of Architectural Historians St. Louis and Missouri Valley Chapters News Letter* 22, 1A (Spring 2019): 1–12.

6   My thanks to Michael E. Willis and Charles E. Fleming for our many conversations about these topics in recent years.

7   Carolyn Hewes Toft with Lynn Josse, *St. Louis: Landmarks and Historic Districts* (St. Louis: Landmarks Association of St. Louis, 2002), 172–73. Aspects of the Homer G. Phillips building were anticipated in Albert Kahn's University (Old Main) Hospital in Ann Arbor, near Detroit; see Michael P. Murphy Jr., et al., *The Architecture of Health: Hospital Design and the Construction of Dignity* (New York: Cooper Hewitt, 2021), 119–24.

8   On Eames's early career in the St. Louis inner suburbs, where he designed a few houses in various, mostly traditional styles, see "Charles and Ray Eames," in John Neuhart, Marilyn Neuhart, and Ray Eames, *Eames Design* (New York: Abrams, 1989), 17–25. Eames and Walsh's Meyer House, designed in consultation with Eliel Saarinen, is also illustrated in Clark, et al., *Design in America*, 86.

9   Nagel later pursued a museum career and served as director of the Saint Louis Art Museum from 1955 to 1964. Dunn's extensive later work includes Faith-Salem Evangelical and Reformed Congregation, Jennings (1951); Steinberg Skating Rink in Forest Park (1957); the National Association of State Garden Clubs Headquarters, St. Louis (1959); and the Lewis and Clark Library (1963; demolished and replaced).

10 See William Barnaby Faherty, *Dream by the River: Two Centuries of Saint Louis Catholicism, 1766–1997* (St. Louis: Archdiocese of St. Louis, 1997), 186–95.

11 "Inside-Out Window," *Time* (December 15, 1952): 84–85. *Time* described this window as "one of the 'boldest' attempts yet in the US to break the mold of traditional design." Cardinal Ritter also rejected Murphy's suggestion, visible on the model, that the belltower of the former church be retained. My thanks to Mary Reid Brunstrom for her research on this and many related topics.

12 Mary M. Stiritz, *St. Louis: Historic Churches and Synagogues* (St. Louis: St. Louis Public Library and Landmarks Association of St. Louis, 1985), 122–23.

13 See Kathleen James-Chakraborty, "Moderate Modernism: Sacred Architecture in St. Louis and its Suburbs" in Mumford, *Modern Architecture in St. Louis,* 26–40; Kathleen James-Chakraborty, "Eric Mendelsohn in America," in Bernd Nicolai, ed. *Architektur und Exil: Kulturtransfer und architektonische Emigration 1930 bis 1950* (Trier: Porta Alba, 2003), 133–43; and Mary Reid Brunstrom, "Bold Modern Form: The Parabola and St. Louis's Sacred Buildings," in Anat Geva, ed., *Modernism and American Mid-20th Century Sacred Architecture* (Abingdon and New York: Routledge, 2019), 73–92. Murphy was dean from 1948 to 1952. The following year he formed a partnership with Eugene J. Mackey Jr., which then became the firm of Murphy and Mackey.

14 Jane King Hession, *The Frank Lloyd Wright House in Ebsworth Park* (St. Louis: The Frank Lloyd Wright House in Ebsworth Park, 2015). Wright also designed a second house in St. Louis County; see Bette Koprivica Pappas, *No Passing Fancy: A Pictorial History of a Usonian Style Home Designed by Frank Lloyd Wright* (St. Louis: Bette K. Pappas, 1995).

15 Jessica Senne, *Suburban Modernism: The Architecture and Interior Design of Ralph and Mary Jane Fournier* (St. Louis: Maryville University, 2014).

16 Bernoudy gave a detailed account of Wright's pedagogy at Taliesin to the Scarab Honor Society at Washington University's School of Architecture in 1936; a transcript on of this lecture is in Osmund Overby, *William Adair Bernoudy: Bringing the Legacy of Frank Lloyd Wright to St. Louis* (Columbia: University of Missouri Press, 1999), 22–25.

17 Ibid., 4–77.

18 Alfred Roth, *The New School* (New York: Praeger, 1953), 183–88.

19 *A Record of the Geodesic Experiment* (St. Louis: Washington University School of Architecture, 1958).

20 Eric Mumford, *The Missouri Botanical Garden Climatron: A Celebration of 50 Years* (St. Louis: Missouri Botanical Garden, c. 2009), 10–57.

21 Robert McCarter, *Aldo van Eyck* (New Haven, CT: Yale University Press, 2015), 116–17.

22 For a summary of Robert Moses's approach to urban renewal, which differed considerably from CIAM's see Susan Fainstein, *The Just City* (Ithaca, NY: Cornell University Press, 2010), 87–89.

23 See my essay "Architectural and Urban Spatial Transformations in St. Louis, 1930s–1970s" in this volume, 55–79.

24 See Michael E. Willis, "A Modernist Memoir Made in St. Louis," in this volume, 147–56, and Ramin Bavar, *LaClede Town* (St. Louis: Washington University School of Architecture thesis, 1994).

25 See Shante Blakely, "The Architecture of Charles E. Fleming," in this volume, 103–23.

Eric Mendelsohn and B'nai Amoona

Kathleen James-Chakraborty

The unequal opportunities available to Black and white immigrants to St. Louis before 1950 are embodied by the former synagogue B'nai Amoona, a Conservative congregation, erected from 1946 to 1950 in University City, an inner-ring suburb of the city of St. Louis. Designed by the German émigré architect Eric Mendelsohn, who had in the 1920s been one of Europe's most influential modern architects before he fled the Nazis, the synagogue represented the cultural as well as spiritual aspirations of its congregants, not to mention their increasingly substantial economic achievements.[1] This came, however, at a time when few new buildings were being built for African Americans, and the boldest new buildings for them would be the high-rise public housing blocks of Pruitt-Igoe, designed by the Japanese-American architect Minoru Yamasaki, a member of another American minority community.

The mobility available to the city's Jewish community encompassed their approach to their own faith, where boundaries between denominations were sometimes fluid. B'nai Amoona was originally the city's only German-speaking Orthodox congregation; many of its more economically successful members eventually joined Reform synagogues. Abraham Halpern, the congregation's rabbi from 1917 to 1962, steered it into Conservative Judaism, the middle ground between these two poles. In 1919 B'nai Amoona moved from the second of the former churches it had occupied to a rather unremarkable building at the intersection of Academy and Vernon Avenues in the city's

West End (fig. 27). This was designed by Alfred Meyer and looked so much like a church that it was later easily sold to the Black congregation of the Holy Metropolitan Baptist Church, the second time that B'nai Amoona passed its house of worship on to African Americans. The additional structures that quickly clustered around this building during B'nai Amoona's occupancy of the site included school and office facilities as well as a library. Within a generation, however, most of those who worshipped at B'nai Amoona had moved further west into University City and beyond, trading the increasingly run-down housing, which included small multifamily dwellings as well as row houses—left behind for their African American neighbors—for more spacious, freestanding, single-family homes.

In the wake of World War II, progress on civil rights came more rapidly for Jews than for African Americans. After the Holocaust, Jews in the United States gained a new measure of acceptance from some of their Christian neighbors.[2] The immediate benefit, for instance, was much greater for them than for African Americans when in 1948 the Supreme Court ruled, in the St. Louis–based case Shelley v. Kraemer, that racially restrictive covenants were unenforceable. Even as Jews still had to campaign for access to the housing, universities, jobs, and leisure facilities available to other whites in St. Louis and elsewhere, many demonstrated a confident commitment to modernism as an aes- thetic choice rather than as something imposed on them by, for instance, a public housing authority and its architects. At the same time, however, many congregations looked inward in the wake of the recent destruction in the Holocaust of the European communities from which their parents, grandparents, and great-grandparents had so recently come. They were also awake to the responsibility that the Shoah placed upon them, as the United States and the fledgling state of Israel replaced Europe and North Africa as the centers of Judaism worldwide.[3] Halpern assured the congregation that the second synagogue building whose construction he oversaw would respond to these new realities.

His focus on the needs of his congregants did not mean by any means that Halpern was indifferent to the concerns of his Black neighbors. In the 1950s, as St. Louis struggled to desegregate, he, like many other rabbis across the country, repeatedly spoke out against the Ku Klux Klan and Jim Crow. In a 1958 sermon, delivered in the building Mendelsohn designed, he declared:

27   Alfred Meyer, former B'nai Amoona
Synagogue, St. Louis, 1919.

*To the prophet all men were equally the children of God and were to be treated
with justice, irrespective of race or color or creed.... But the world today
refuses to accept this truth and continues to hold to the anti-religious concept
of race superiority. This brings into full focus the tragedy of Jim Crowism that
is practiced so unjustly even in our own country. To me Jim Crowism is most
revolting, and is all the more so when practiced by most churches and
institutions of learning. It is a horrid manifestation of a distorted conception
of religion. The courageous stand by [Catholic] Archbishop [Joseph] Ritter
of our city is an oasis that must be emulated by all religious leaders.*[4]

The reference—to Ritter's insistence on integrating the archdiocese's schools—was not a unique example of interfaith solidarity
in the city. Not only would B'nai Amoona write a new page in the
history of the architecture of synagogues in the United States;
its impact on the architecture of Christian churches, many
of them Catholic, across the St. Louis metropolitan area was yet
another signal of Jewish integration into the white mainstream.

Eric Mendelsohn and St. Louis

Erich Mendelsohn (he and his wife anglicized their names following their departure from Germany in 1933, with her changing from Luise to Louise) was born in 1887 in the then-German city of Allenstein (now Polish Olsztyn). At the age of thirty-four he became famous within Germany following the 1921 publication on the cover of the weekly magazine *Berliner Illustrirte Zeitung* of what was then the still unfurnished shell of the Einstein Tower, located in Potsdam, just southeast of Berlin.[5] His design for this solar telescope was the most startling manifestation of the short-lived vogue for Expressionist architecture that swept through avant-garde German architectural culture immediately after the end of the war. Mendelsohn quickly regrouped, however, designing far more pragmatic and yet urbane structures with streamlined curves that captured the new technological spirit of speeding motor cars and safety razors. These had an almost immediate nearly global impact, with apartment blocks, cinemas, office towers, and department stores showing his influence.

In 1933 the architect fled Nazi Germany for London and then Jerusalem before departing in 1941 for the United States, to which he had first traveled in 1924.[6] Upon his arrival he was quickly granted an exhibition at the Museum of Modern Art in New York. Its impact, however, was muted by the attack on Pearl Harbor. A few years later, in 1944, the show traveled to St. Louis (fig. 28). Mendelsohn's connections there included his former German client Erwin Weichmann (later Winston), for whom he had built a small store in the then-German city of Gleiwitz (now Polish Gliwice). Other allies were the lawyer Victor Packman; Gilbert Harris of the local YMCA; Charles Nagel Jr., the director of the City Art Museum (now the Saint Louis Art Museum), which hosted the exhibition; and Joseph D. Murphy, the future dean of architecture at Washington University, as well as various notables from the city government and the business community. When he visited the city in conjunction with the exhibition, Mendelsohn, who had not yet received any commissions in the United States, aspired to a professorship at Washington University and a role in the city's urban planning efforts, but he had already identified synagogue design as a possible, if less exciting, way to relaunch a career that had hitherto been dominated by secular work.

ERIC MENDELSOHN, European architect, mounting his own
exhibit in building design for display at the City Art Museum.

28   Eric Mendelsohn installing his exhibition,
Architecture by Eric Mendelsohn, 1914–1940, at the City
Art Museum (now the Saint Louis Art Museum), 1944,
from an article in the *St. Louis Star-Times*.

From St. Louis he traveled to Davenport, Iowa, to discuss a synagogue project that never materialized. In Davenport he noted
"no racial restrictions, antisemitism scarcely present as at St. Lou s."
From there he went to Omaha, where he was hosted, as in
Iowa, by a local rabbi interested in a new building.[7] Mendelsohn
returned briefly to St. Louis in June of 1945. With the war finally
over and congregations in a position to make concrete plans,
he was back again by the end of October, this time to meet B'nai
Amoona's building committee, which had already purchased
a site in 1942.[8] The result would be the architect's first commission since his arrival in the United States four years earlier.

Mendelsohn's first building had been a chapel oui t in 1913
for the Jewish cemetery in his native Allenstein, and although
religious structures comprised a relatively minor part of his
subsequent practice, he continued until his departure in 1933
to design synagogues and other buildings for Jewish congregations in Germany, where modern architecture was not an

unusual choice during the 1920s.[9] Although most of these were destroyed as a result of the Nazi's anti-Jewish pogroms during Kristallnacht in 1938, they established his reputation for Jewish congregations in the United States as the world's most celebrated Jewish architect. For many, it was also an advantage that he was a dedicated Zionist, whose commissions in British Mandate Palestine included a hospital for Hadassah, the American women's organization that was active in many Jewish congregations.[10]

Although Mendelsohn brought significant experience to his work in the US, he in no way repeated his earlier work. He produced an entirely new conception for B'nai Amoona, one that also differed from his later American synagogue schemes, each of which was carefully tailored to the conditions of its own site.[11] Although Mendelsohn's major English work, the De la Warr Pavilion in Bexhill-on-Sea of 1935, was much of a piece with his German commercial work, his buildings in Mandatory Palestine erected across the course of the following five years exhibited his willingness to begin again by paying meticulous attention to local conditions. The United States, with the world's most advanced construction industry, which had already inspired him on his first visit to the country, was yet another very different situation that had little in common with the project of establishing a Jewish homeland in relation to Arab building traditions that Mendelsohn very much respected.

Designing B'nai Amoona

The challenges Mendelsohn faced with the B'nai Amoona synagogue were multiple. First, what direction should postwar synagogue design take to address the specific circumstances of the country's increasingly prosperous and assimilated Jewish communities? Second, in what direction would his own architecture evolve in relation to very different conditions from those in which he had already built in Europe and in Palestine? While it is not clear that conditions specific to St. Louis, aside from the details of the site itself, informed these choices, certainly Mendelsohn attempted to integrate into an architectural culture which he saw in terms of Frank Lloyd Wright, Eliel Saarinen, and William Wurster, more than his fellow German émigrés Walter Gropius and Ludwig Mies van der Rohe.

B'nai Amoona pioneered a new approach to synagogue design, one that he advanced in the plans of his subsequent synagogues for Cleveland Heights, Grand Rapids, and St. Paul, even as he developed entirely new compositions for each. Mendelsohn defined his approach in an article published in 1947:

[Our] temples should reject the anachronistic representation of God as a feudal lord, should apply contemporary building styles and architectural conceptions to make God's house a part of the democratic community in which he dwells. Temples should reject in their interiors the mystifying darkness of an illiterate time and should place their faith in the light of day. The House of God should either be an inspiring place for festive occasions that lift up the heart of man, or an animated gathering place for a fellowship warming man's thoughts and intentions by the fires of the divine word given forth from altar and pulpit right in their midst.[12]

Such a synagogue made a dramatic break with the many larger and much more richly decorated neo-Byzantine temples erected across the country in the 1920s by prosperous Reform and Conservative congregations. Mendelsohn's site on the corner of Trinity and Washington Avenues lay just over a mile from one such building, United Hebrew Temple (now the Missouri Historical Society Library and Research Center) prominently located on Skinker Boulevard. Erected in 1924 by Maritz & Young with Gabriel Ferrand, this Reform synagogue—an excellent example of the type—was a point of reference for Mendelsohn only in one later project and then only obliquely, the Park Synagogue in Cleveland Heights, whose domed sanctuary he designed after B'nai Amoona but which was largely completed earlier.[13] Although B'nai Amoona occupied a less prominent site and was not as imposing as United Hebrew, its emphatically modern appearance, shorn of all historical references, pointed toward the future rather than the past. Moreover, while United Hebrew had faced lawsuits from Christian neighbors seeking to prevent the congregation from building on such a prominent site, in more progressive postwar conditions B'nai Amoona faced no such obstacles.[14]

Mendelsohn's design process began, as was characteristic for him, with perspective drawings (fig. 29). Although he always designed in careful relationship to a building's site, overt reference to the site was almost never part of the drawings. In the case of B'nai Amoona he treated a largely residential suburban setting, in which many might have chosen to pull the mass of the building well back from the street, as a relatively urban one. A model, photographed as if an aerial view (fig. 30), made clear the juxtaposition of masses he envisioned, even as the project was built in stages. While the drawings show the building from the right side of the main entrance, and thus focus on the volume of the sanctuary, the angle of the photograph of the model shows the opposite side, allowing the viewer to fully comprehend the layout of the ancillary spaces. While focusing on the exterior massing, Mendelsohn also carefully balanced the building's public presence with the way in which it would function for its users.

From its beginnings in the 1910s, Conservative Judaism in the United States privileged the provision of education and social facilities that nurtured a sense of community.[15] This would prove key to Mendelsohn's understanding of the synagogue in his new

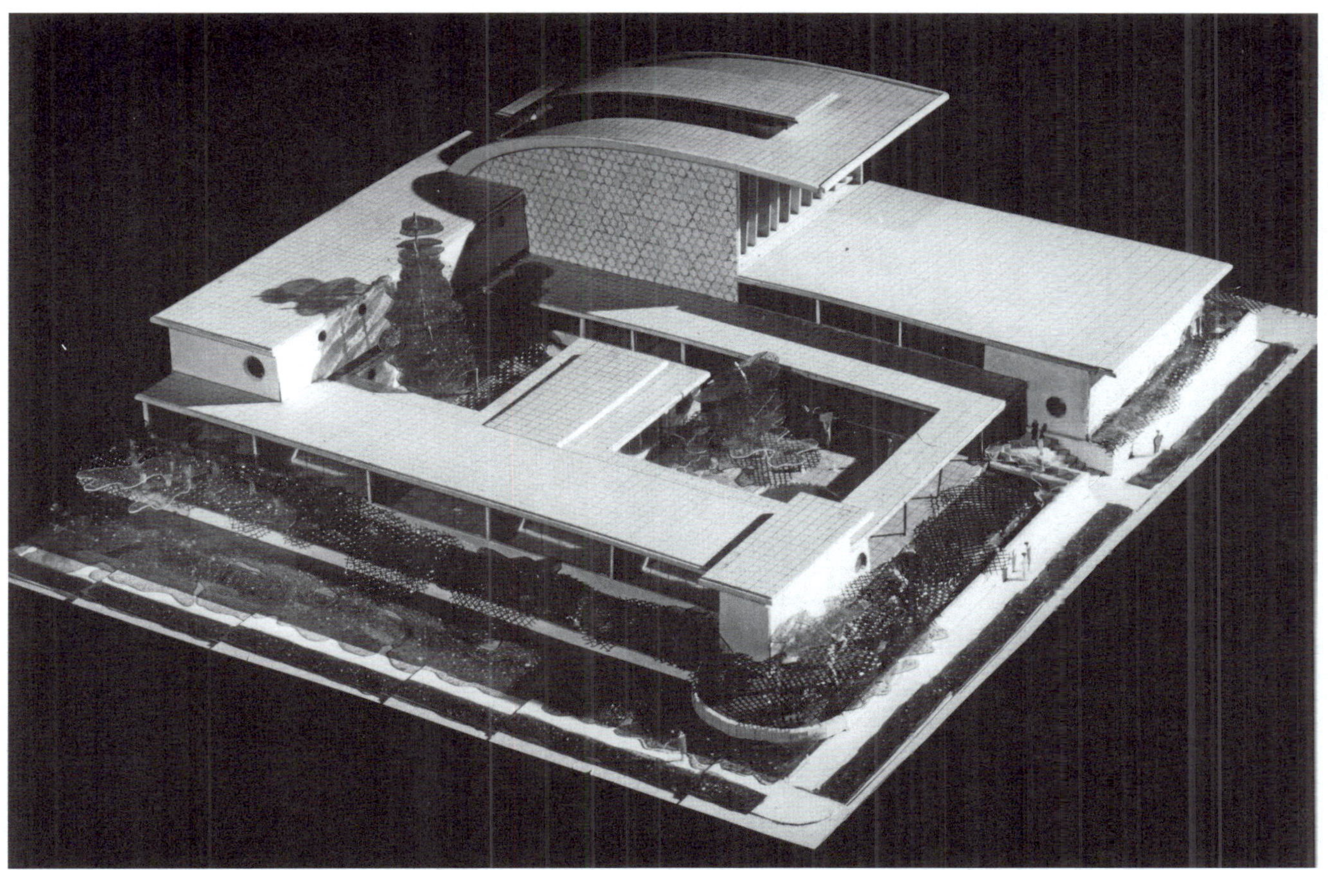

30　Eric Mendelsohn, B'nai Amoona Synagogue and Community
Center, 1946–50, University City, Missouri, model 1947.

homeland, even when building for Reform congregations. One
outcome of the Holocaust was a greater commitment on the
part of assimilated Jews across the country to establish a sheltered environment in which children could meet each other
while learning Hebrew and the tenets of their faith, and in which
adults could relax together, network, and raise funds in support
of Israel and local charities.[16] In addition to the temple, a smaller
chapel, and offices for the rabbi and his staff, B'nai Amoona
contained classrooms and a social hall complete with kitchen
facilities. The social hall was separated from the sanctuary
by a folding wall, allowing the temple space to be easily
expanded on High Holy Days, an arrangement Mendelsohn
repeated in all of his other synagogues.

Key to the construction of the building (fig. 31) was the participation of the contractor, Isadore E. Millstone.[17] Millstone learned
about Mendelsohn while a student at Washington University
in the mid-1920s.[18] Although he himself was a member of United

31 Construction of the B'nai Amoona sanctuary, 1946–50, University City, photograph 1949.

Hebrew Congregation, for which his father had worked, he never faltered in his commitment to B'nai Amoona, later helping to fund its conversion into the Center of Creative Arts (COCA), which he also helped oversee. While Mendelsohn had not built in the United States before and did not fully understand local construction practices, Millstone, who had been in business since 1927, was able to guide him. Millstone must also have admired Halpern, whose strong commitment to civil rights he shared. He worked to ensure that Blacks were not shut out of St. Louis construction unions and that they received the training necessary to join them. It also helped that Millstone shared Mendelsohn's Zionism and his commitment to modern architecture.[19] He accompanied Louis Kahn on a trip to Israel shortly after it achieved independence, where they strategized about how to house its refugee population.

The Place of B'nai Amoona in Postwar Architecture

Mendelsohn's achievement garnered enormous positive attention for B'nai Amoona both locally and nationally.[20] The building's bold forms, clad in a warm orange-tan brick, mediated effectively between the radical innovations he had helped pioneer in Germany in the 1920s and midcentury modern architecture in the United States, especially the work of Frank Lloyd Wright and Eliel Saarinen (figs. 32, 33). In the wake of its completion, the modernist synagogue and the community buildings that supported it became showcases of up-to-the-minute architectural thinking across the country, while in the St. Louis metropolitan area B'nai Amoona's presence kicked off a series of innovative church designs, including by Mendelsohn's friend Joseph Murphy and the young Gyo Obata.

In 1945 the Finnish-born Saarinen was still the most prominent European émigré architect practicing in the US. In 1942 Saarinen, to whom Mendelsohn was first introduced in 1924 on the same trip on which he became acquainted with Wright, completed the First Christian Church in Columbus, Indiana (see fig. 12), one of the most modern religious structures erected in the country.[21] The same year the two architects had dinner together in Detroit.[22] Although B'nai Amoona ostensibly resembled First Christian only in its use of brick, the presence in Columbus of a classroom block organized around an interior courtyard established a typological similarity between the two complexes.

B'nai Amoona sparked a golden age in synagogue design in the United States, one which would see high-profile buildings by major architects, including Wright's celebrated Beth Shalom completed outside Philadelphia in 1959 and such other groundbreaking facilities for Jewish communities as Louis Kahn's iconic 1955 bath house at the Trenton Jewish Community Center. A new generation of Jewish-American architects—including Richard Meier, who curated an exhibition on the subject at the Jewish Museum in New York in 1963, and Peter Eisenman, who traveled to St. Louis to see B'nai Amoona shortly after its

32   Eric Mendelsohn, B'nai Amoona Synagogue
and Community Center, University City,
Missouri, 1946–50.

33   Eric Mendelsohn, B'nai Amoona Synagogue
and Community Center, University City,
Missouri, 1946–50, sanctuary.

completion—was inspired by Mendelsohn's example, even though synagogue design played little role in their work.[23] Arguably just as important was the more low-key work of Percival Goodman as well as the many local architects whose synagogues were outstanding examples of the modern architecture emerging in suburbs from coast to coast.[24]

B'nai Amoona also inspired the erection of modernist churches throughout the St. Louis metropolitan area, as white Christians joined Jews in reimagining the appearance of sacred space.[25] Murphy, for example, enjoyed the support of Archbishop Ritter in the series of churches he designed in the 1950s that followed Mendelsohn's example and that of pioneering German church designers such as Dominikus Böhm. All of Murphy's designs shared with Böhm's churches and Mendelsohn's synagogues the undivided spaces believed to foster an empathetic sense of community among congregants.[26]

The most important exponent of modern religious architecture in the St. Louis metropolitan area was Gyo Obata, who designed both synagogues and churches, at least one of which was clearly influenced by Mendelsohn's example. The Abbey Church at Saint Louis Priory School (Priory Chapel) in the Creve Coeur suburb of St. Louis (see figs. 39, 52–54), consecrated in 1962, was developed in part out of Obata's admiration for Mendelsohn's unbuilt design for a Baltimore synagogue.[27] Equally important, however, was the degree to which the presence of B'nai Amoona convinced clients from across the region that modern designs could be both practical and prestigious.

This project has received funding from the European Research Council (ERC) under the European Union's Horizon 2020 research and innovation programme (grant agreement No. 101019419).
For a fuller explication of Mendelsohn's B'nai Amoona project, see my book *In the Spirit of Our Age: Eric Mendelsohn's B'nai Amoona Synagogue* (St. Louis: Missouri Historical Society, 2000), from which much of this essay is derived.

1   Rachel Kranson, *Ambivalent Embrace: Jewish Upward Mobility in Postwar America* (Chapel Hill: University of North Carolina Press, 2017), 3.

2   Ibid.

3   See Israel Goldstein, "American Jewry Comes of Age," *B'nai Amoona Sixtieth Jubilee* (St. Louis: B'nai Amoona, 1942), unpaginated, for a statement of this position even before the extent of the Holocaust then underway had become clear. See also Kranson, *Ambivalent Embrace*, 6.

4   Bernard S. Raskas, ed., *A Son of Faith: From the Sermons of Abraham E. Halpern, 1891–1962* (New York: Bloch Publishing Company, 1962), 39. Lila Corwin Berman, in her *Metropolitan Jews: Politics, Race and Religion in Postwar Detroit* (Chicago: University of Chicago Press, 2015), details the engagement of Detroit's Jewish leadership, including its rabbis, in civil rights efforts, as well as the tensions this generated within the Jewish community.

5   *Berliner Illustrirte Zeitung*, September 4, 1921, cover.

6   For more on Mendelsohn, see Kathleen James, *Erich Mendelsohn and the Architecture of German Modernism* (Cambridge: Cambridge University Press, 1997); Regina Stephan, ed., *Eric Mendelsohn: Architect, 1887–1953* (New York: Monacelli, 1999); Bruno Zevi, *Erich Mendelsohn: Complete Works* (Basel, Switzerland: Birkhäuser, 1999); and Carsten Krohn and Michele Stavagna, *Erich Mendelsohn: Buildings and Projects* (Basel, Switzerland: Birkhäuser, 2022).

7   Eric Mendelsohn, letter to Louise Mendelsohn, March 16, 1944, Erich Mendelsohn Archive, Die Briefwechsel von Erich und Luise Mendelsohn, 1910-1953, Kunstbibliothek, Staatliche Museen zu Berlin, accessed July 30, 2022, http://ema.smb.museum/de/briefe.

8   Mendelsohn's wife, Louise, later remembered that he had made contact with Halpern through the Austrian writer René Fülöp-Miller, who spent part of the war years at the same farm north of New York City. Annotation to Erich Mendelsohn's letter to Louise Mendelsohn, March 6, 1944, Erich Mendelsohn Archive, accessed July 30, 2022, http://ema.smb.museum/de/briefe.

9   See my essay "Small Buildings for the Jewish Communities in Tilsit, Königsberg and Essen," in Stephan, *Erich Mendelsohn: Architect*, 167–77; and Carol Hershelle Krinsky, *Synagogues of Europe: Architecture, History, Meaning* (Cambridge, MA: MIT Press, 1985), 93–96, 302–9.

10   Ita Heinze-Mühleib, *Erich Mendelsohn: Bauten und Projekte in Palastina (1934–1941)* (Munich: Scaneg, 1986).

11   See Walter C. Leedy Jr., *Eric Mendelsohn's Park Synagogue: Architecture and Community*, ed. Sara Jane Pearman (Kent, OH: Kent State University Press, 2012); see also Michael Craig Palmer, *Eric Mendelsohn's Synagogues in America* (London: Lund Humphries, 2019).

12   Eric Mendelsohn, "In the Spirit of Our Age," *Commentary* 3 (1947): 541.

13   For the history of American synagogue architecture, see Sam Gruber, *American Synagogues: A Century of Architecture and Jewish Community* (New York: Rizzoli, 2003); and Rachel Wischnitzer, *Synagogue Architecture in the United States: History and Interpretation* (Philadelphia: Jewish Publication Society of America, 1955).

14   "History," United Hebrew Congregation (website), accessed July 14, 2022, https://www.unitedhebrew.org/about/history/.

15   See David Kaufman, *Shul with a Pool: The "Synagogue Center" in American Jewish History* (Waltham, MA: Brandeis University Press, 1999).

16   See Edward S. Shapiro, *A Time for Healing: American Jewry since World War II* (Baltimore: Johns Hopkins Press, 1992).

17   For an overview of Millstone's impact on St. Louis, see Dirk Johnson, "A Suicide at 102 Unites a City in Thanks for a Man's Life," *New York Times*, June 16, 2009, https://www.nytimes.com/2009/06/16/us/16millstone.html.

18   Isadore E. Millstone, interview with the author, June 1998.

19   Susan G. Solomon, *Louis I. Kahn's Trenton Jewish Community Center* (New York: Princeton Architectural Press, 2000).

20   See for example Robert E. Hannon, "Contemporary Synagogue: A Structure by a Famous Architect and for University City Congregation," *St. Louis Post-Dispatch*, December 24, 1950, Pictures Supplement, 5; and "Synagogue in St. Louis," *Architectural Forum* 98 (April 1953): 109–15.

21   Albert Christ-Janer, *Eliel Saarinen: Finnish-American Architect and Educator* (Chicago: University of Chicago Press, 1979), 88–92, 97–101.

22   Eric Mendelsohn, letter to Louise Mendelsohn, March 19, 1942, Erich Mendelsohn Archive, accessed July 14, 2022, http://ema.smb.museum/de/briefe/?id=1245.

23   Richard Meier, *Recent American Synagogues* (New York: The Jewish Museum, 1963), which republished Mendelsohn's article for *Commentary*. Steven Skrainka, interview with the author, June 1998, for Peter Eisenman's interest in B'nai Amoona.

24   Kimberly J. Elman and Angela Giral, eds., *Percival Goodman: Architect, Planner, Teacher, Painter* (New York: Miriam and Ira D. Wallach Art Gallery, Columbia University, 2001). Later synagogues in the region designed by notable modern architects include Congregation Temple Israel in Creve Coeur (Gyo Obata, 1962); Shaare Zedek in St. Louis (Bernard Bloom, 1950); and United Hebrew in Chesterfield (Pietro Belluschi, 1989).

25   See my essay "Moderate Modernism: Sacred Architecture in St. Louis and Its Suburbs," in Eric Mumford, ed., *Modern Architecture in St. Louis: Washington University and Postwar American Architecture, 1948–1973* (St. Louis: Washington University School of Architecture, 2004), 27–40.

26   Kathleen James-Chakraborty, *German Architecture for a Mass Audience* (London: Routledge, 2000), 63–69.

27   For more on Gyo Obata, see Winifred Elysse Newman's essay "Gyo Obata's 'Other' Modernism" in this volume, 81–101.

Architectural and Urban Spatial Transformations in St. Louis, 1930s–1970s

Eric P. Mumford

In the 1930s St. Louis was one of the world's major industrial and corporate centers, ranked ninth in "value added by manufacture" among cities in the United States.[1] Like other North American metropolitan regions at that time, it was still substantially rail oriented. It was also where many of the six million African Americans, moving north in the first Great Migration (1910–40) to escape the oppressive racial hierarchies in the South, found new homes, albeit in a racially segregated and unequal environment. Since the nineteenth century St. Louis had also been a haven for European immigrants fleeing sociopolitical oppression in their own homelands. Many of these immigrants had acquired considerable wealth and exerted cultural influence in their new surroundings, mostly living within ten miles of downtown St. Louis.

34   Map of Mill Creek Valley land uses, from Virginia
Anne Henry, "The Sequent Occupance of Mill Creek Valley,"
master's thesis, Washington University, 1947.

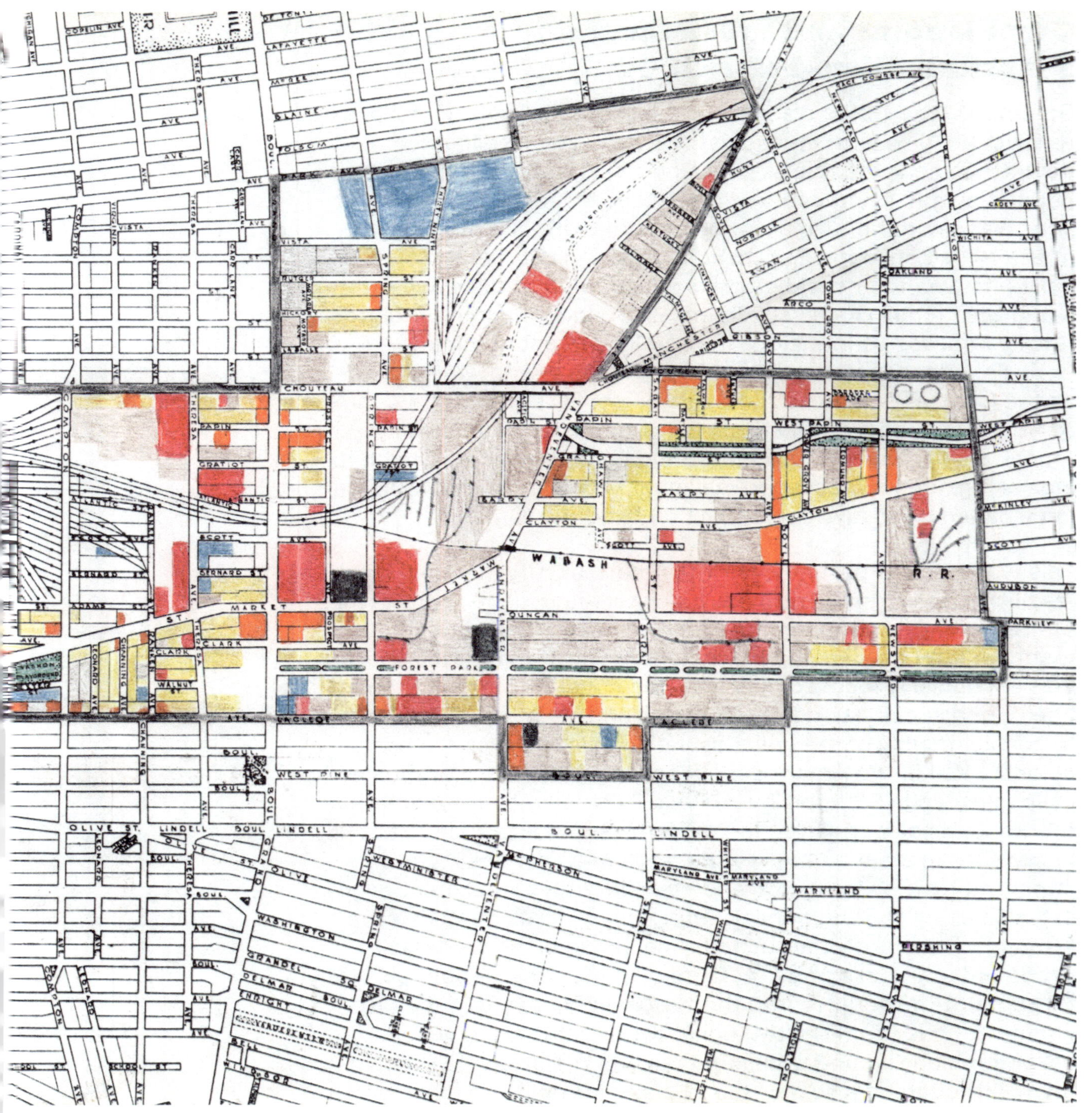

City Planning and Urban Spatial Transformations before 1940

St. Louis in the 1930s was one of the most centralized of North American cities, with most of its major businesses located downtown near the Mississippi River, and the majority of its population still living within a few miles, mostly along streetcar lines. Yet since the turn of the twentieth century—the period of the 1904 Louisiana Purchase Exposition (St. Louis World's Fair)—its wealthier residents were beginning to move west along the Lindell Boulevard "central corridor," building architecturally impressive mansions in racially and economically exclusionary private streets, primarily in what was later known as the Central West End. In this same context, the Civic League of St. Louis published the first regional master plan for an American city in 1907, which resulted in neoclassical civic buildings along a new landscaped mall near City Hall downtown and landscaped parkways ringing the city and the region.[2]

This was also the period when the American city planning profession began to emerge, inspired by the landscape architecture of Frederick Law Olmsted, the American City Beautiful movement, and the garden city movement in Great Britain. The latter was particularly focused on improving conditions affecting the health and social harmony of the working class, then understood to consist mainly of the white racial groups in Europe and its colonies and in the Americas. These directions were enthusiastically taken up in St. Louis by Harland Bartholomew, appointed the St. Louis city engineer in 1916, who soon became a nationally known urban planner. Most of Bartholomew's plans involved improved traffic circulation and were intended to protect property values by limiting nonresidential uses in residential areas. Although they rarely mentioned race, these plans were also produced in the era of de facto segregation that would persist throughout the country into the 1960s. In his work as the city engineer, he is prominently known for his 1947 plan, which called for clearing and rebuilding most of the areas near downtown, although he also developed plans for new suburban areas, including University City (1922, 1931), Clayton (1928), Ferguson (1931), and Ladue (1937).[3]

For Bartholomew, following on the ideas of Olmsted and aspects of the garden city movement, "comprehensive planning" involved working with private business interests in determining the location and layout of new streets, buildings, parks, schools, and commercial areas to produce legally binding city plans, with little or no input from area residents. City planners of this era also were critical of previous US urban patterns, as these usually lacked landscaped open spaces, often used grid plans, were not designed for cars, and were denser and more mixed-use than early-twentieth-century elites thought was desirable.

Such older urban areas typically surrounded downtowns, and by the 1910s they began to be deemed "blighted," a term then defined as areas where real estate values were flat or declining, often because of the influx of heavy industry and the presence of "inharmonious groups." In St. Louis such an area in the central part of the city was Mill Creek Valley, located east of Grand Boulevard to Twentieth Street, south of Olive Street and Lindell Boulevard, and north of Scott Street (figs. 34–36). This was a dense, mixed-use area that included both once-luxurious mansions and townhouses, mostly from the late nineteenth century, churches, and commercial streets, much like other parts of the central city. The houses, built before indoor plumbing or electricity, had lost their appeal by the early 1910s, and the expansion of heavy industry was making the area unhealthy for residential uses.[4] Yet along with the more well-established Ville area, Mill Creek Valley was also one of the few parts of the city where Black residents arriving in the first years of the Great Migration could find rental housing, often near factory and domestic service jobs, usually in old houses that had been subdivided into apartments. An entertainment district, Chestnut Valley, emerged there, as did such Black institutions as Vashon High School (1927), whose original building is now part of Harris-Stowe State University, and churches, banks, theaters, and the Pine Street YMCA (1919).[5]

In 1912, even as this vital Black community was developing, efforts were made to clear part of the area for a new "Central Traffic-Parkway"—similar to ones in other cities designed by Olmsted and by the Kansas City city planner George E. Kessler—that would allow affluent residents of the West End to drive their new cars from their private streets to their downtown offices, anticipating much later mid-twentieth-century highway planning. In the same decade, which was also when city voters passed a racial segregation ordinance (1916), Bartholomew began to identify other blighted areas within the older residential parts of the city, notably in the DeSoto-Carr area north

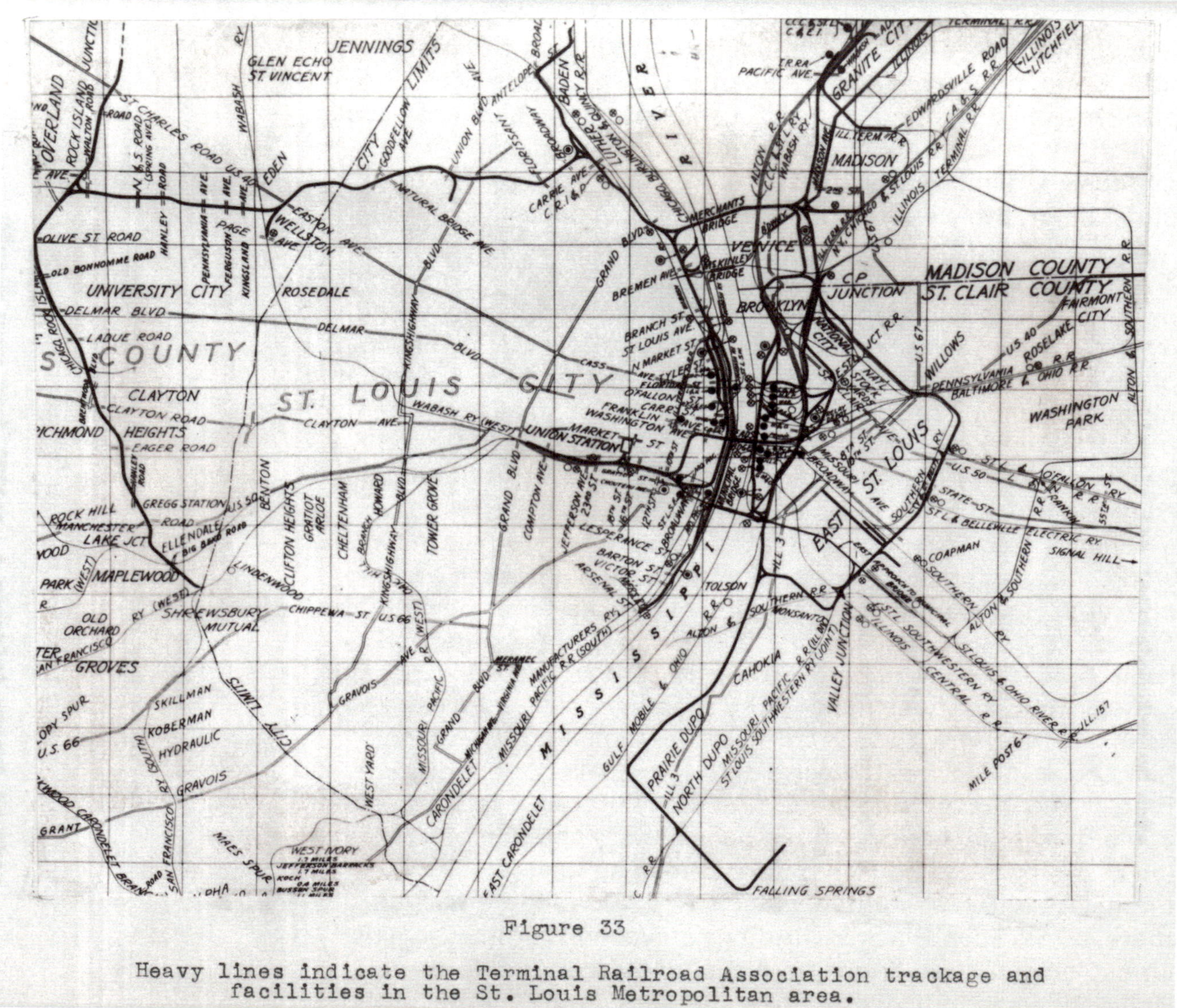

Figure 33

Heavy lines indicate the Terminal Railroad Association trackage and facilities in the St. Louis Metropolitan area.

35 Map of St. Louis terminal railroad lines, from Virginia Anne Henry, "The Sequent Occupance of Mill Creek Valley," master's thesis, Washington University, 1947.

36 Aerial view of Mill Creek Valley before clearance, 1959.

of downtown. By 1928 he also proposed that the old riverfront be cleared to make way for business towers and a sunken expressway; this foreshadowed some of what would be built there in the 1960s in relation to the Jefferson National Expansion Monument (JNEM, commonly known as the Gateway Arch).

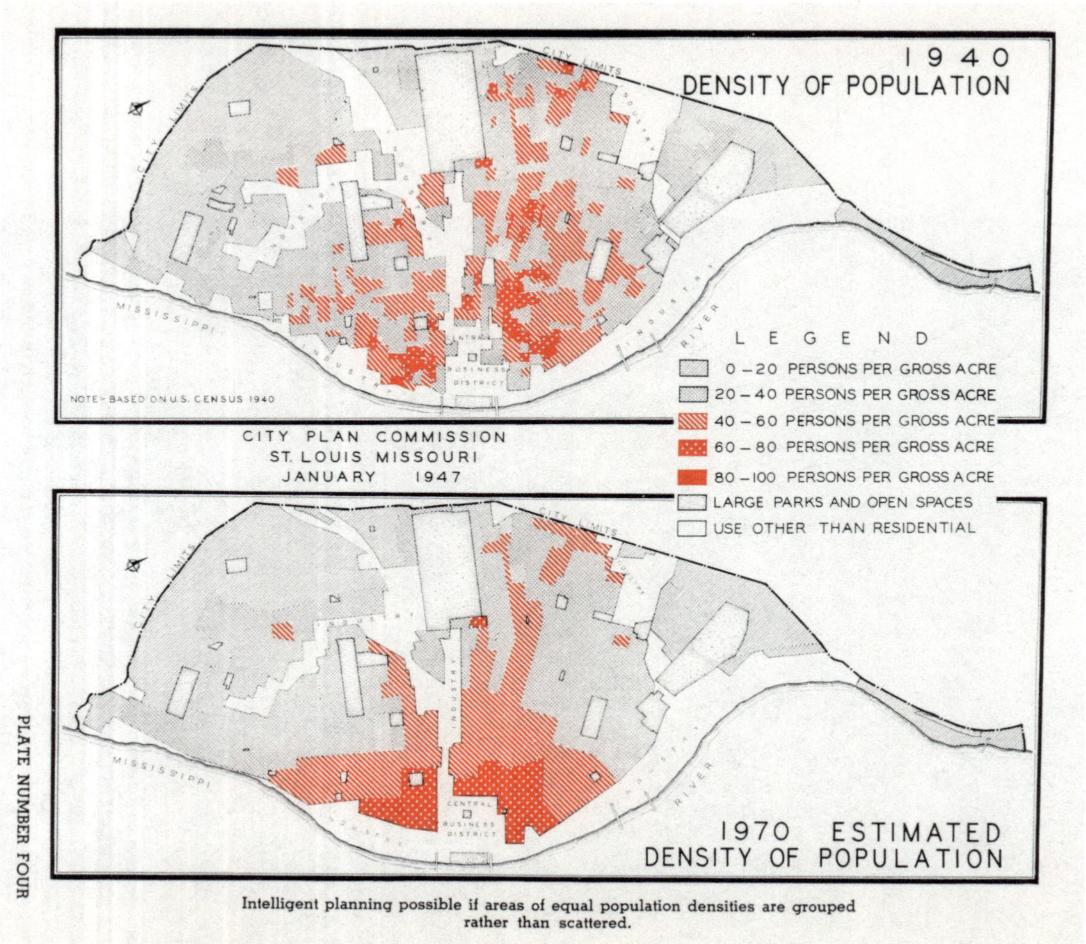

37   Harland Bartholomew and Associates, map of 1940–1970 projected population growth of St. Louis, 1947.

In the early 1930s these efforts to clear and rebuild led to the development and construction of Neighborhood Gardens (1934), at 1204 North Eighth Street, a 252-unit subsidized housing project with community facilities for white working-class residents, supported by private philanthropy and located on blocks that had been declared blighted by the City Plan Commission. Inspired by European social housing, it soon became a national redevelopment housing model, as the federal government under the New Deal embarked on the funding of public housing projects across the country, beginning with two in New York City in 1934. These housing projects were required to follow the "neighborhood composition rule," which forbade building new housing in blighted areas for people who were of a different race than the existing residents. In St. Louis the first two public housing projects, Clinton-Peabody (1941) for white residents and Carr Square Village (1942) for Black residents, clearly demonstrated the impact of this national policy, which remained in effect until 1954.[6]

Modern Architecture Becomes Mainstream in St. Louis, 1947–1965

Federal funds in the 1930s were also made available for extensive highway and other infrastructure construction, much of it intended to both provide jobs for the unemployed and decentralize industry and workers in line with planning ideas of the garden city movement. By 1940 the US census showed for the first time a slight decline in the city's population, intensifying civic leaders' concerns that St. Louis was losing its position as one of the largest American cities, even as its residential and industrial outskirts were growing (fig. 37).

In response, a coalition of business leaders including Joseph Pulitzer Jr., the publisher of the nationally influential *St. Louis Post-Dispatch* newspaper, and Morton D. May, an executive of the May Department Stores Company, then a leading national department store chain, convinced Mayor Aloys P. Kaufmann to commission Bartholomew to prepare plans to reconstruct the central city in what was thought to be an effective way to counter suburban migration, similar to what Robert Moses, New York City's construction coordinator, was then doing in New York. Bartholomew's 1947 Comprehensive City Plan assumed that the city's population would continue to grow, but it also assumed (without mentioning it directly) the retention of existing patterns of de facto segregation, which then strictly limited public accommodations and residential areas open to African Americans.[7] The proposal included demolishing and rebuilding crowded older areas near downtown, providing new low- and high-rise apartment housing and new highways in the process. A clear outcome of these efforts was the eventual displacement of the growing Black population from the old residential and industrial areas near downtown.

The way these urban reform ideas, especially regarding clearance
and rebuilding, could lead to a modern postwar city was also
evident in the national architectural competition to design the
Jefferson National Expansion Memorial on the downtown
riverfront, commemorating President Thomas Jefferson's vision
of the continental expansion of the United States, as well as
recognizing the site's importance as the "gateway to the West"
for the westward expansion of mostly white settlements.
Declared a National Historic Site in 1935, the riverfront land
was cleared in 1939–41, with the idea that a neoclassical monument like the recent George Rogers Clark Memorial (1929)
in Vincennes, Indiana, would be built there with federal support.[8]
Preparing the site was the next step in clearing "obsolete" areas
near downtown, which then still housed some 175 Black and
white residents amid mostly commercial buildings, many of historical and architectural significance. After its clearance the site
served as a parking lot for the downtown department stores
and other uses until around 1960. A national design competition
for the memorial was held in 1947–48, supported by Luther Ely
Smith, a local lawyer and civic activist, May, and other city leaders.
The winning design, chosen by a national jury that included the
West Coast modern architects Richard Neutra, William Wurster,
and others, was by Eero Saarinen, the son of the Finnish-American
architect and educator Eliel Saarinen, with landscape design
by Dan Kiley. It was one of the first departures from Beaux-Arts
classical monumentality in American urban design.[9]

The selection of the Gateway Arch in this competition marked
the end of neoclassicism in American civic design and its
replacement (at least until the 1980s) by modern architecture.
Modern architecture was a twentieth-century effort to efficiently
use new building technologies and new architectural strategies
to transform daily life and, especially in its early stages, to
improve basic living conditions for the urban working classes.
It was based on a quasi-scientific belief system, and after 1932
it was offered as a design strategy worldwide, potentially usable
by any regime regardless of its politics. It was nonetheless
mostly forbidden in the USSR from 1932 to 1954 and in Nazi
Germany. After 1945 modern architecture began to be widely
used internationally, including in the USSR after the Soviet dicta-
tor Joseph Stalin's death in 1953. It also became politically
controversial in the US in the late 1940s, after Saarinen's JNEM
design was selected, in part because of the Arch design's associa-
tions with European fascism and internationalism generally.

Despite these objections, the enthusiastic local, national, and international response to the outcome of the JNEM competition in 1948 was paralleled by more extensive local institutional patronage for modern architecture, which had begun in the 1930s. The results after World War II included architecturally prominent religious, civic, and commercial buildings, primarily in the suburbs, but also some within the city limits.[10] Civic and commercial buildings that used modern design ideas were highly visible throughout the region by the 1950s, including Harris Armstrong's American Stove Company building (later Magic Chef; 1946–47, see figs. 5, 6; altered) with its molded-plaster lobby ceiling by Isamu Noguchi, and the new terminal for Lambert–St. Louis Airport (1950–56, later St. Louis Lambert International Airport; figs. 38, 48, 49) designed by Minoru Yamasaki, a Detroit-based Japanese-American architect whose partners at the time were Joseph Leinweber of Detroit and George Hellmuth of St. Louis.[11] Yamasaki's assistant on the project, the architect Gyo Obata, had narrowly avoided being sent to an internment camp in 1942, like his Japanese-American parents and most Japanese-Americans on the West Coast, by attending the School of Architecture at Washington University in St. Louis. He then went on to found the internationally recognized St. Louis firm Hellmuth, Obata + Kassabaum (HOK) in 1956, with George Hellmuth from the Yamasaki firm. Inspired by the work of the Italian architect Pier Luigi Nervi, Obata designed the thin-shell, vaulted, concrete Priory Chapel (1956–62; see figs. 39, 52–54) at the Saint Louis Priory School in the suburb of Creve Coeur, as well as many other locally and nationally prominent architectural works.[12]

Highly visible other midcentury works include Steinberg Skating Rink (1957), an ice-skating rink in the largest public park in the city, by Frederick Wallace Dunn and Nolan Stinson; Mark C. Steinberg Hall (1960; see fig. 24) on Washington University's campus by the then-young faculty member Fumihiko Maki; and the James S. McDonnell Planetarium (1963; see figs. 55, 56) by HOK. Until 2006 Steinberg Hall housed the University's art collection (now the Mildred Lane Kemper Art Museum) and the Department of Art History & Archaeology.[13] Around the same time the Missouri Botanical Garden, after considering relocating to the suburbs, decided to remain in the city and embark on an ambitious effort to modernize its facilities. The centerpiece of these efforts was the Climatron (1960; see fig. 25), the world's first geodesic dome greenhouse, designed by Murphy and Mackey with Synergetics Inc., a firm founded by Buckminster Fuller.

38 Hellmuth, Yamasaki + Leinweber,
Lambert-St. Louis Airport, 1950–56,
exterior side view.

39 Gyo Obata / Hellmuth, Obata + Kassabaum (HOK) the Abbey Church, Saint Louis Priory School (Priory Chapel), Creve Coeur, Missouri, 1956–62, aerial view.

These architectural works were produced at the same time
as large slum-clearance public housing projects began to be built
near downtown following Bartholomew's 1947 plan, beginning
with the white-only Cochran Gardens (1948; demolished),
a high-rise project by Hellmuth and Yamasaki sited adjacent
to Neighborhood Gardens, and continuing with the Wendell O.
Pruitt Homes and William Igoe Apartments, known as Pruitt-Igoe,
located on North Jefferson Avenue between Carr Street and
Cass Avenue, extending east to North Twentieth Street (fig. 40).

40   Hellmuth, Yamasaki + Leinweber, the Wendell O. Pruitt Homes
and William Igoe Apartments complex, St. Louis, 1950–56.

Reflecting emerging concerns about de facto segregation after
the 1948 Shelley v. Kraemer Supreme Court decision, which had
ruled that racially restrictive property deed riders were unconstitutional and could not be legally enforced, the white-only Igoe
project was located north of the Black-only Pruitt project, with
the idea that children from both would use the same play-
grounds.[14] At the same time, the white-only Darst-Webbe public
housing project was constructed on the Near Southside, east
of Lafayette Square. In 1954 racial segregation in public housing

and public schools was ruled unconstitutional, and the last of these five large high-rise projects—the George L. Vaughn apartments (1957–2006) just east of Pruitt-Igoe—was expected to be integrated.

A year later, in 1955, a city bond issue was passed by voters by a large margin, with the backing of a new, local, big-business coalition, Civic Progress, founded two years earlier. This funded the modernization of much of the city's infrastructure, including parks, schools, and highways. The routing of the new interstate highways through the city, additionally funded in 1956 by the federal government, was deliberately used to clear areas Bartholomew had identified in the 1947 plan as blighted. These included Interstates 55 and 44 on the south, Interstate 70 on the north, and Interstate 64 / Highway 40 north of Chouteau Avenue, displacing residents and businesses along the way (fig. 41).

Seeking a Racially Integrated Region through Design, 1963–73

The 1955 bond issue also funded the clearance and rebuilding of Mill Creek Valley. This displaced some 19,700 residents, about 95% Black, from one of the two major centers of Black life in the St. Louis region, the other being the Ville neighborhood in North St. Louis. As with the other "urban renewal" projects of this period, the clearance and rebuilding of Mill Creek Valley also had the enthusiastic support of the mostly white building trade unions in the city, as well as some mainstream Black organizations, such as the Urban League and the NAACP, who were concerned about the bad living conditions there. Although a considerable amount of new housing was built, including the racially integrated LaClede Town (1963, figs. 44, 88, 89; demolished), designed by Chloethiel Woodard Smith, a pioneering woman modern architect based in Washington, DC, many of the former Mill Creek Valley residents moved to existing housing in North St. Louis. During this same period other areas near downtown were cleared as well, including the mostly white Kosciusko neighborhood on the Mississippi River, south of downtown and east of Soulard, which was then rebuilt as a new industrial area. This was also the period of the middle-income redevelopment of the area near Union Station, just west of downtown, for the Plaza Square development, designed by HOK and Harris Armstrong (figs. 42, 87).

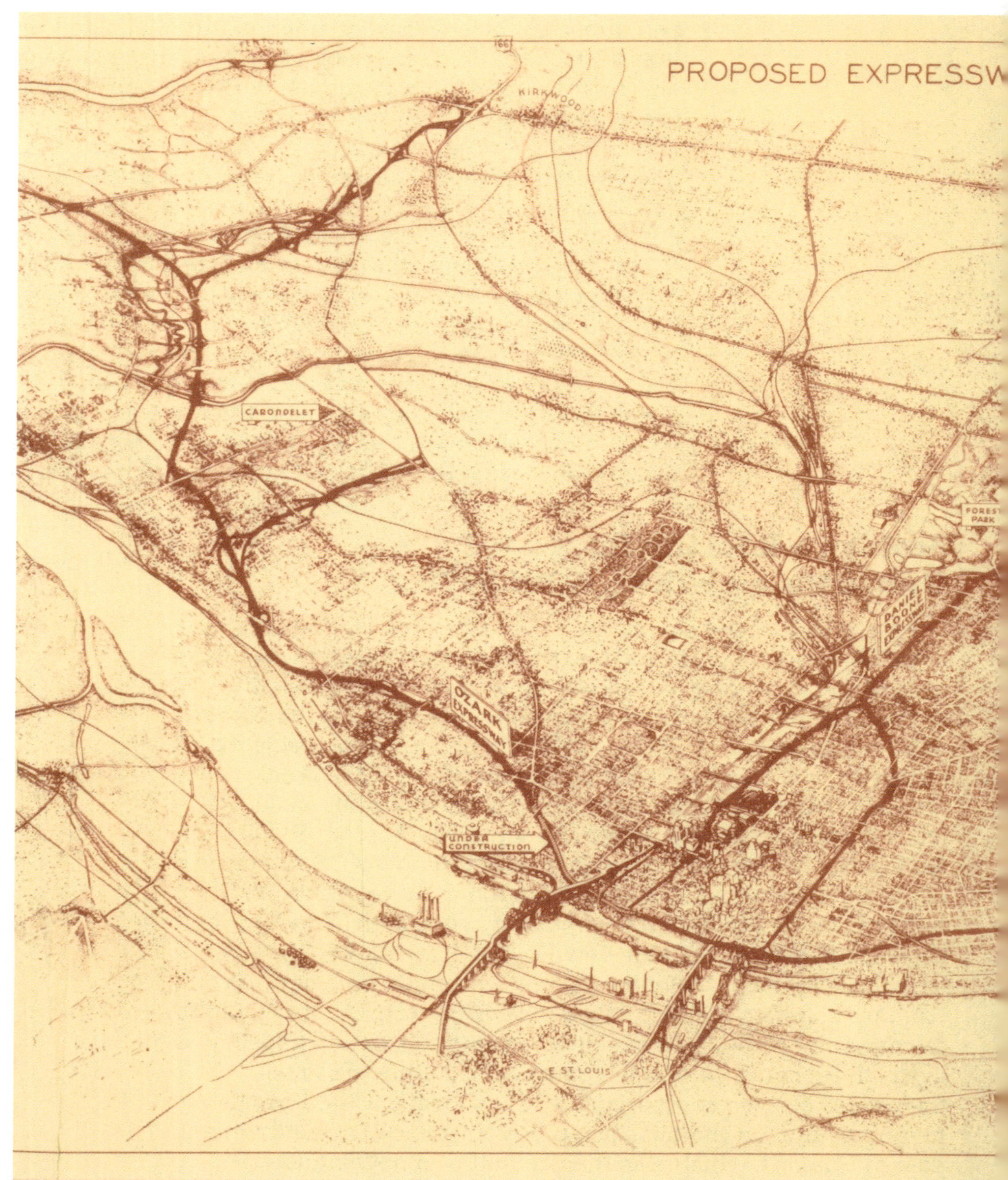

41   City of St. Louis Mayor's Office,
proposed express highway plan, 1953.

...TEM FOR THE ST. LOUIS AREA
ST. CHARLES
LAMBERT FIELD
MARK TWAIN EXPRESSWAY
BADEN
MADISON
GRANITE CITY
JOE RAY

Near the end of this period of both urban destruction and ambitious new modern design, Saarinen's 630-foot-tall stainless steel Gateway Arch was finally completed in 1965, thirty years after the New Deal creation of a riverfront park and monument. When the Arch opened, its intended symbolism of American westward expansion was just beginning to be questioned; now it is often seen as a gesture celebrating the triumphant white erasure of Indigenous people and Black urban life.

42   Harris Armstrong and Hellmuth, Obata + Kassabaum (HOK), Plaza Square, St. Louis, 1957–61.

By the mid-1960s the implementation of federal laws prohibiting racially segregated schools and public housing had led to extensive "white flight" from the city by those who wanted to avoid living in racially integrated communities. New houses, schools, and religious buildings began to appear in the rapidly developing and racially homogenous suburban areas, now served by the new interstates. While these were not officially designated for whites only, Black buyers and other ethnic minorities were blocked via various direct and indirect means from purchasing homes or land in these areas, leaving only the remaining older inner-city neighborhoods for their use.[15] The "Delmar Divide," named after the major east-west street that separates North St.

Louis from the rest of the city, emerged during this time, as the previously mostly white (and racially exclusionary) Northside became briefly integrated, then nearly all Black by the 1960s. A similar divide formed in the adjacent suburbs—more or less along Olive Boulevard, another prominent east–west corridor—separating white communities from incoming Black homebuyers, usually with limited incomes.[16]

Around the same time, as racial segregation was being made illegal nationally during the 1954-68 period, the many social and design shortcomings of large modern housing projects like Pruitt-Igoe also began to be sharply criticized. Roger Montgomery, then a professor at the Washington University School of Architecture, who also cofounded the Landmarks Association of St. Louis in 1958, began to champion both racial integration and better design in federally funded subsidized housing.[17] A new urban agenda was promoted by a younger generation of activists and architects, including Montgomery and Charles E. Fleming, Washington University's first Black graduate in architecture, who received his degree from Washington University's University College in 1961. Influenced by the sociological studies of Oscar Newman, whose theories, initially based on research at Pruitt-Igoe, focused on the relation of architectural design to crime, these emerging designers ultimately rejected high-rise slum clearance as an urban solution and advocated instead for racially integrated townhouse developments.[18]

In the cleared Mill Creek Valley, some small, racially integrated, experimental projects were built. These included both conventional modernist mixed-use developments like Council Plaza (1964–68), designed by the firm Schwarz and Van Hoefen with Richard Henmi for the local Teamsters union, with its distinctive "saucer" (originally a Phillips 66 gas station; fig. 43), and Woodard Smith's more experimental LaClede Town. It was also at LaClede Town, sited south of Olive Street between Compton Avenue and North Ewing Street, that important connections were made between the artists of the Black Artists' Group and jazz musicians, including some of the members of what became the World Saxophone Quartet.[19]

A few years later, the internationally known East St. Louis–based Black choreographer and educator Katherine Dunham commissioned Buckminster Fuller to design Old Man River's City, a visionary mixed-use residential and industrial megastructure

43   Richard Henmi, Schwarz and Van Hoefen,
former Phillips 66 gas station , 1968 ("the saucer"),
in Council Plaza, St. Louis, 1964–68.

Page 78
44   Chloethiel Woodard Smith, LaClede Town,
St. Louis, 1963.

on the east side of the Mississippi River (1970–73, see figs. 72, 74–84; unbuilt).[20] Around this same time, during and just after the national Great Society period of federal reforms addressing racial inequalities in the 1960s, a new city administration began to empower Black professionals in civic work, including Fleming.[21] Fleming's contributions to the design and building history of St. Louis—mostly unrecognized until recently—include numerous works from the 1960s and 1970s, such as the St. Louis Comprehensive Neighborhood Health Center (1974; see fig. 26) and the renovation of many city parks, most of them designed when he was a partner in the national firm of Jenkins-Fleming Inc. from 1968 to 1979.[22]

By the mid-1970s, after the demolition of Pruitt-Igoe (1972–76), the value of historic urban neighborhoods began to be reconsidered, which led to the creation of the St. Louis Development Corporation in 1974. Washington University, for example, decided to keep its medical campus in the Central West End rather than move it to west St. Louis County, as many other institutions were then doing.[23] Historic preservation, transit planning, and the provision of urban amenities began to replace slum clearance and public housing as the main focus of urban planning efforts.[24] Many areas declared to be obsolete in the 1947 plan, such as the neighborhoods of Lafayette Park and St. Louis Place, resisted a proposed new urban interstate highway in the late 1970s that would have cleared both; they continue to be centers of urban life in the city today.

In 1977 the Harvard-educated British architect and critic Charles Jencks declared that the first demolitions at Pruitt-Igoe in 1972 marked the symbolic "death of modern architecture" and its utopian aspirations.[25] International debates followed as to the reasons why Pruitt-Igoe had been a failure, some of them ill-informed about local circumstances, and became part of the widespread rejection of modern architecture by the 1980s and later, especially in North America and Great Britain.[26] The Pruitt-Igoe site remained vacant into the 2010s, and the project has continues to be a powerful symbol of the failed urban planning of this era. At the same time, many of the works of modern architecture produced in St. Louis in the mid-twentieth century are now much admired and sometimes highly valued, even as the now-sprawling metropolitan region continues to change.

1 For a general history of St. Louis from its founding to 1980, see James Neal Primm, *Lion of the Valley: St. Louis, Missouri, 1764–1980*, 3rd ed. (St. Louis: Missouri Historical Society, 1998).

2 Mark Abbott, "A Document That Changed America: The 1907 *A City Plan for St. Louis*," in Mark Tranel, ed., *St. Louis Plans: The Ideal and the Real St. Louis* (St. Louis: Missouri Historical Society, 2007), 17–53.

3 "Alphabetical Listing of Comprehensive Plans," Eldridge Lovelace, *Harland Bartholomew: His Contributions to American Urban Planning* (Urbana: University of Illinois, 1993), Appendix A-15-19, https://www.stlouis-mo.gov/archive/harland-bartholomew/.

4 See Virginia Anne Henry, "The Sequent Occupance of Mill Creek Valley" (master's thesis, Washington University, 1947), https://doi.org/10.7936/69b2-y272. The use of the term "blighted" in relation to St. Louis and Mill Creek Valley's declining property values is discussed in detail in St. Louis City Plan Commission, *St. Louis Central Traffic-Parkway* (St. Louis: City Plan Commission, 1912), 5–21.

5 John A. Wright, *Discovering African-American St. Louis: A Guide to Historic Sites*, 1st ed. (St. Louis: Missouri Historical Society, 1994), 23–42.

6 On Neighborhood Gardens and early St Louis public housing, see Joseph Heathcott, "'In the Nature of a Clinic': The Design of Early Public Housing in St. Louis," *Journal of the Society of Architectural Historians* 70, no. 1 (March 2011): 82–103. On the political and racial context of these directions, see Clarence Lang, *Grassroots at the Gateway: Class Politics and Black Freedom Struggle in St. Louis, 1936–75* (Ann Arbor: University of Michigan Press, 2009), 17–96.

7 St. Louis City Plan Commission and Harland Bartholomew and Associates, *Comprehensive City Plan: St. Louis, Missouri* (St. Louis: City Plan Commission, 1947), https://www.stlouis-mo.gov/archive/1947-comprehensive-plan/index.shtml. On the influence of the New York example in St. Louis planning in the 1940s, see Alexander von Hoffman, "Why They Built Pruitt-Igoe," in *From Tenements to the Taylor Homes: In Search of Urban Housing Policy in Twentieth-Century America*, ed. John F. Bauman, Roger Biles, and Kristin M. Szylvian (University Park: Pennsylvania State Press, 2000), 180–205. The history of how racial integration was achieved in St. Louis is briefly traced in Amanda E. Doyle and Melanie A. Adams, *Standing Up for Civil Rights in St. Louis* (St. Louis: Missouri Historical Society, 2017).

8 Robert J. Moore Jr., *The Gateway Arch: An Architectural Dream* (St. Louis: Jefferson National Parks Association, 2005), 12–23.

9 Moore, *The Gateway Arch,* 24–43.

10 Mary Reid Brunstrom, "Four Decades of Modern Architecture in St. Louis, 1928–1968: An Expanded View" and "The Gateway Arch: St. Louis's Modernist Signature," in *St. Louis Modern*, ed. David Conradsen and Genevieve Cortinovis (St. Louis: Saint Louis Art Museum, 2016), 10–53.

11 "Progress in St. Louis," *Architectural Forum* 18, no. 4 (October 1948): 70–79; and Dale Allen Gyure, *Minoru Yamasaki: Humanist Architecture for a Modernist World* (New Haven and London: Yale University Press, 2017), 17–38; Daniel L. Rust, *The Aerial Crossroads of America: St. Louis's Lambert Airport* (St. Louis: Missouri Historical Society, 2016).

12 Walter McQuade, *Architecture in the Real World: The Work of HOK* (New York: Harry N. Abrams, 1984), 9–21 and 180–83; see also Gyo Obata, "Memoir," in *Modern Architecture in St. Louis: Washington University and Postwar American Architecture, 1948–1973*, ed. Eric Mumford (St. Louis: Washington University School of Architecture, 2004), 84–89.

13 Both Steinberg Skating Rink and Steinberg Hall were gifts of Etta Eiseman Steinberg, a St. Louis philanthropist and art collector. See Elizabeth C. Childs, "St. Louis and Arts Philanthropy at Midcentury: The Case of Etta E. Steinberg," Mildred Lane Kemper Art Museum (website), https://www.kemperartmuseum.wustl.edu/research/historical-research/the-case-of-etta-e-steinberg.

14 Bob Hansman, *Pruitt-Igoe* (Charleston, SC: Arcadia, 2017).

15 The many phases of spatial segregation in St. Louis city and county are traced in detail in Colin Gordon, *Mapping Decline: St. Louis and the Fate of the American City* (Philadelphia: University of Pennsylvania Press, 2008).

16 The first houses sold to Black buyers in University City were on Forest Green Court in 1965. See Judy Little with Esley Hamilton, *University City: Landmarks and Historic Places* (University City, MO: 1997), 31.

17 University of California, Berkeley, College of Environmental Design, *Roger Montgomery (1925–2003), Celebration and Memorial, Wurster Hall, November 13, 2004*, memorial brochure.

18 Oscar Newman, *Defensible Space: People and Design in the Violent City* (London: Architectural Press, 1972). Also see Roger Montgomery, "Pruitt-Igoe: Policy Failure or Societal Symptom," in *The Metropolitan Midwest: Policy Problems and Prospects for Change* (Urbana: University of Illinois Press, 1985), 229–43. Montgomery questioned Newman's "architectural determinism" as to why Pruitt-Igoe was a failure.

19 Ramin Bavar "LaClede Town: An Analysis of Design and Government Policies in a Government-Sponsored Project" (master's thesis, Washington University School of Architecture, 1995); Benjamin Looker, *"Point from Which Creation Begins": The Black Artists' Group of St. Louis* (St. Louis: Missouri Historical Society, 2004). For a personal reflection on growing up in LaClede Town, see Michael E. Willis, "A Modernist Memoir Made in St. Louis," in this volume, 147–56.

20 For more on Old Man River's City, see John C. Guenther, "Buckminster Fuller's Old Man River's City: A Visionary City Unrealized," in this volume, 125–45.

21 Between 1964 and 1969, President Lyndon B. Johnson's administration enacted the "Great Society" programs, significant urban reforms that required massive federal spending to remedy some of the outcomes of structural racism in cities. See Wendell E. Pritchett, *Robert Clifton Weaver and the American City: The Life and Times of an Urban Reformer* (Chicago: University of Chicago Press, 2008), 246–352. Weaver was the first secretary of the newly created Department of Housing and Urban Development (HUD), serving from 1966 to 1968, and the first Black cabinet member in US history.

22 For more on Fleming's career, see Shantel Blakely, "The Architecture of Charles E. Fleming," in this volume, 103–23.

23 Interview by the author with Donald Royse, professor emeritus, Washington University, St. Louis, 1997.

24 An example of the new positive attitude toward historic preservation in the 1970s is the exhibition catalog by James Marchael and George McCue, *The Architecture of St. Louis* (St. Louis: City Art Museum, 1971).

25 Charles Jencks, *The Language of Post-Modern Architecture* (New York: Rizzoli, 1977), 9.

26 Katharine G. Bristol, "The Pruitt-Igoe Myth," *Journal of Architectural Education* 44, no. 3 (May 1991): 163–71.

Gyo Obata's "Other" Modernism

Winifred Elysse Newman

Born in 1923, Gyo Obata came of age as an architect in the mid-twentieth century. Ten years after he was born, the Congrès Internationaux d'Architecture Moderne (CIAM: International Congresses of Modern Architecture), whose members authored modernist manifestoes, held its fourth conference culminating in a meeting not far from the Parthenon. By the time Obata enrolled in the University of California, Berkeley, in 1941, modernism was firmly established as a style and a lifestyle aligned with contemporary values around progress through technology, efficiency, and what was soon to be buoyant postwar capitalism.

CIAM included the first generation of "modernist" architects, primarily born in Europe at the end of the nineteenth century. Such figures as Charles-Édouard Jeanneret, known as Le Corbusier, Walter Gropius, Richard Neutra, J. J. P. Oud, and Ludwig Mies van der Rohe were promoted in the American context in the 1932 Museum of Modern Art's *Modern Architecture: International Exhibition*, and the simultaneously published book by Henry-Russell Hitchcock Jr. and Philip Johnson, *The International Style: Architecture since 1922.*[1] Rather than a representative catalog, this was a primer for an emerging "international" style, focusing on specific characteristics of its leading European examples. The rules promoted by Hitchcock and Johnson unmoored architecture from the masonry and stone buildings of the previous generations. In their view architecture should be lightweight, glassy, formal, and, most importantly, functional, without applied ornament. Imposing the rules onto existing buildings, however, did more than identify commonalities in a genre; it set the terms to which all modern buildings must adhere and forced the conceptual complexity of their ontological functionalism into its opposite—a style. This code meant a design should look like a modern building regardless of specific context or locale.

In his 1995 publication *The Other Tradition of Modern Architecture*, the British architect and historian Colin St John Wilson argued for a social countertradition to modernism.[2] Wilson critiqued modernist architecture's mainstream orthodoxy as part of the cult of the CIAM personalities led by Le Corbusier, although also including the communist architects André Lurçat, Hannes Meyer, Hans Schmidt, and Mart Stam. Wilson's accusation that a small club of "conspirators" determined the rules for everyone else still resonates for some. Wilson offered a way out of a singular and stylistic conception of modernism. He posited an "other" coeval modernism, rooted in an idiosyncratic humanist approach similar to Hugo Häring's argument early in CIAM for "building organically" regarding the balance of nature and man's responsibility.[3] For architecture this meant allowing for the irrational, the imperfect, and the performance of emergent complexity to shape form. Le Corbusier (and CIAM) promoted a humanism still rooted in the imposition of man's will through order—the architect as a Platonic philosopher-king bringing order out of the chaos that is man's natural state, as in the classical tradition of architecture.

Many of Gyo Obata's midcentury projects develop this notion of a parallel yet distinct modernism akin to Wilson's idiosyncratic humanism. A close look at three of them—Lambert–St. Louis Airport terminal, Priory Chapel, and the James S. McDonnell Planetarium—provides a nuanced appreciation of the difference between high modernism's stylistic characteristics and a building's purpose attuned to human activities. The ambiguous or even contradictory expressions of the genre in the three buildings, like Wilson's small club, challenge the idea that there was or is a singular modernism in architecture. These outliers in the modernist canon are part of our lived experience, but we tend to undervalue what does not fit clearly into a conceptual mold.

Background

One challenge in researching Obata's work is the scant written record regarding his design philosophy. Books and articles with interviews or quotes repeat the similar refrain that the design should evolve "directly from the requirements of a building. . . at the same time complementing and respecting the environment" and include "customizing for each client and his needs."[4] But as an explanandum, these do little to unpack the *why* of his designs.[5] The best clues to that are in "St. Louis, A Study in Urban Decay" (1946), Obata's graduate school thesis written for his Master of Arts in Architecture and Urban Design at the Cranbrook Academy of Art in Bloomfield Hills, Michigan.

By the time Obata completed his undergraduate studies at UC Berkeley, prejudices toward Japanese Americans stemming from Japan's role in World War II culminated in their incarceration in concentration camps on the West Coast; Obata took the train east to the first university that accepted him, the School of Architecture at Washington University in St. Louis. Immediately upon graduation he enrolled at Cranbrook, where Eliel Saarinen was the director. Obata's thesis under Saarinen echoes CIAM's modernist trope of efficiency and zoned, hierarchical planning, from the scale of the neighborhood to the township, city, and, finally, the entire economic region. Still, it also stresses Saarinen's belief that collective action and community are at the city's heart.[6] Obata focuses on "planning for the needs of the people," which he pairs with the idea that "if our society is going to survive, man must improve spiritually and culturally to narrow this discrepancy between the physical, scientific and social sciences." Technocratic planning of the kind advocated by CIAM with its "unintegrated living, working, and transportation functions only confuses and frustrates man. . . . [We] must plan our cities for human beings."[7]

This interest in communal urban experience is more akin to what Wilson termed the "human functionalism" of the other modernism as reflected in the work of Häring as well as Alvar Aalto, Eileen Gray, and Hans Scharoun, among other architects. This additional modernism shares similar aspirations with CIAM. For instance, in reaction to the suggestion that standardization and industrial building methods were a natural response to economic need, Gray and Jean Badovici countered, "We must build for people so that they can find once more in architecture the job of enlarged powers and self-fulfillment."[8]

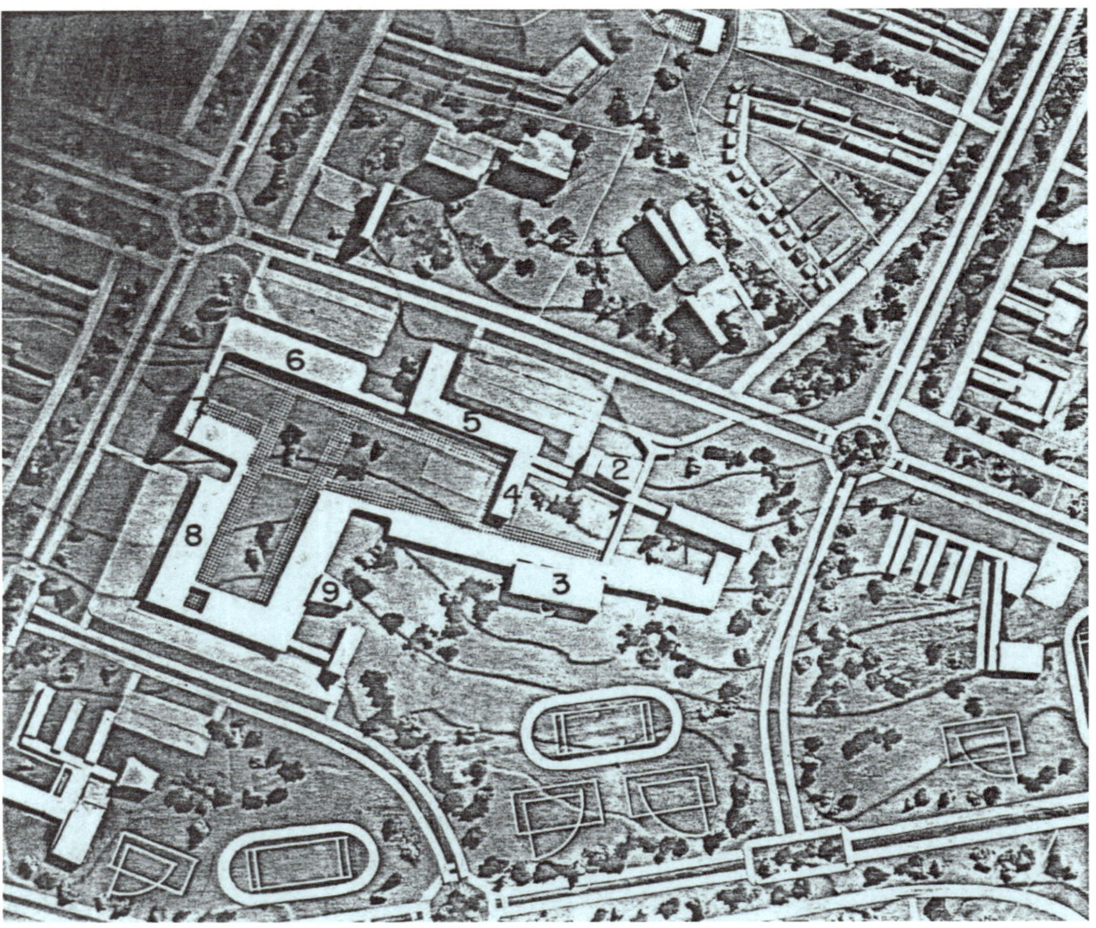

45   Township nucleus map, from Gyo Obata, "St. Louis, A Study
in Urban Design," master's thesis, Cranbrook Academy of Art, 1946.

Where CIAM urbanism breaks the city into discreet units of working, living, and playing, linked with the connective tissue of transportation without attention to the civic identity of inhabitants connected to shared public spaces, Obata proposed an urban renewal plan for St. Louis organized around a township unit with a green center supporting a robust communal identity. He notes in his thesis, "An urban community developed along this line will indeed be an organic social structure. It will give man the opportunity for better social intercourse and cultural and physical development" (fig. 45).[9] Echoing Gray, he argued that the responsiveness of this organic social structure "counters the current material culture informed by science and technology, shaping society and the environment."[10] This position contradicts the general prewar modernist ethos that embraced the possibilities of technology and science expressed through a functional architecture organized according to rational standardization and mass-production principles. Although his thesis project was never built, later work by Obata as part of the firm Hellmuth, Obata + Kassabaum (HOK), especially a series of school campus projects, echoes this same communal focus, with classrooms or offices organized around central spaces scaled for small group interactions. These include the Bristol Elementary School (1956) in suburban St. Louis (fig. 46); the IBM Advanced Systems Development Laboratories at Los Gatos, California (1965; fig. 47); and Xerox PARC (Palo Alto Research Center) for IBM (1970).

46   Hellmuth, Obata + Kassabaum (HOK), Bristol Elementary School, Webster Groves, Missouri, 1956.

The imagery and formulation of functional modernism originating with CIAM, championed by Hitchcock and Johnson and promoted in such magazines as *Progressive Architecture* and *Architectural Record*, persisted into the late mid-twentieth century. What critics responded to in Obata's midcentury work was its stylistic resonance with modernism, what the architectural historian Karl Bötticher in the eighteenth century termed *Kunstform*, or formal, aesthetic appearance of a building. Bötticher paired this with the idea of the *Kernform*, or inherent properties of a building.[11] I am suggesting that the traditional appearance of Obata's work in the midcentury is comfortably modernist, but the kernel motivating the design was his interest in the occupant's experience. The need for a more human-centered architecture is part of a concurrent counter-movement manifesto by design groups such as Team 10 in Europe but somewhat ignored by American critics and the popular press.

47   Hellmuth, Obata + Kassabaum (HOK), IBM Advanced Systems Development Laboratories, Los Gatos, California, 1964.

Lambert–St. Louis Airport

The idea of spaces designed to accommodate social interaction finds resonance with one of Obata's first projects working as Minoru Yamasaki's assistant at Hellmuth, Yamasaki + Leinweber: the Lambert–St. Louis Airport terminal (1950–56; see figs. 38, 48, 49). Ten years older than Obata, Yamasaki was also from California, nisei, and his career followed a similar trajectory. The design team, including the airport consulting firm Landrum & Brown, analyzed the program and prepared a report outlining their approach. Airports were a relatively new building type in the 1950s. The report stressed the functional performance guided by three criteria: maximize comfort, convenience, and efficiency throughout all airport services. Given the growing passenger demand, the other crucial issue was designing for expansion. The proposed plan connected three large vaults (each 120 square feet by 32 feet high) linearly, with a single outdoor passenger concourse running perpendicular to the terminal (fig. 48). This scheme made expansion straightforward: extend the airport and add more vaults.

48 Hellmuth, Yamasaki + Leinweber, Lambert-St. Louis Airport terminal, 1950–56, model 1952.

For Yamasaki, the design concept for the airport was more than tactical functionality. It harkened back to Grand Central Station in New York City, which he saw as a "Gateway to the City," with all the excitement of arrival and departure amid the hustle and bustle of human activity.[12] He wanted the St. Louis terminal building to feature a similar "great room." The designers,

49   Hellmuth, Yamasaki + Leinweber, Lambert–St. Louis Airport terminal, 1950–56, photograph by Ezra Stoller / Esto Photographics Inc.

based in part on the experience of the engineer Anton Tedesko, turned to thin-shell concrete domes to provide flexibility and achieve an uninterrupted space 412 feet long and 120 feet wide.[13] Thin-shell concrete was an experimental and, at the time, underused structural solution. There were only two similar roof structures: Eero Saarinen's Kresge Auditorium at MIT (1950–55) and Matthew Nowicki's J. S. Dorton Arena in Raleigh, North Carolina (1949–52). This solution employed apparent aspects of American architectural "opticalism" that used visible technical innovation to signify prestige.[14] The Lambert design married the thin-shell concrete vaults to commercial plane travel, an exciting midcentury innovation. Yamasaki's later "roof buildings," including the West Gymnasium at Carleton College and Temple Beth El in Bloomfield Hills, Michigan, also employ the roof as a focal point over a single space. Still, compared to the airport terminal, these projects were relatively simple in their spatial configuration.

Although Lambert's functional requirements were more complex than worship spaces or auditoriums, that alone did not account for the spatially dense organization of the program.

Airport consultants at the time recommended the "unit system," where separate facilities housed all the needed services for each airline. The disadvantage to this plan was that it required long connecting corridors with no central collection point for flight information.[15] The solution at Lambert is surprisingly sectional, with functions organized on three levels. The flow from ticketing to boarding is visible and experienced linearly by passengers (fig. 49). This sectional organization and complexity may be the influence of Yamasaki's project assistant, Gyo Obata.[16] The Obata House on Greeley Ave (1954) displays a similar section. The entry is at the midpoint between the basement level and the first floor, adding dynamism to the entry sequence and visual interest to the front facade (fig. 50).

50   Gyo Obata, Obata residence, Webster Groves, Missouri, 1954.

At Lambert the main departure floor is roofed by three, later four, cylindrical groined vaults scaled to feel inviting rather than overwhelming. Ticketing for all carriers is handled in the main hall. Passengers proceed down one level to the concourse, and in several areas, the two levels are open to each other. This organization adds to the excitement of the overall complex and helps clarify the flow of arriving and departing passengers. From the terminal's "great space," passengers have a panoramic view of the runways and aprons, which were the point of access to the planes during the age of propeller planes. Initially, the complex included a 500-foot-long spectator deck extending out from the terminal over the central concourse, increasing the perception of the connection between the "great space" and the tarmac, much like the connection between the great hall and the train platforms at New York's Grand Central Station. This approach focuses on the human experience over the functionality of the airport. As noted earlier, the optimal design for functionality uses the "unit system" that prioritizes the carrier's operational functions over the passenger experience. For the Lambert design, however, the passenger experience informs the entire spatial configuration of the airport, from the point of departure in the "great hall" to the tarmac and onto the plane. The spectator deck enables passengers and those accompanying them to participate in the farewell ritual and emphasizes the social experience of travel more than the technological one.

In contrast to this is Eero Saarinen's TWA Terminal at Idlewild Airport in New York (1954, later John F. Kennedy International Airport; fig. 51). The openness of the views from the interior to the exterior in the main terminal similarly highlights the experience of being at the airport. Still, unlike Lambert, passengers transition to gates in satellite structures built on the runaways remote from the terminal. This organization optimizes the management of equipment and baggage handling—that is, the functionality of airport operations is paramount to the now segregated departure experience of the traveler.

The *Kunstform* of Lambert and TWA exemplifies the New Sensualism in modernism first noted by Thomas Creighton. The term Creighton applied to the TWA Terminal—Romantic Expressionism—was, as he saw it, a retreat from modernism into a plastic-sculptural-emotional architecture where functions are fitted into the space.[17] The danger, for Creighton, of New Sensualism's mix of intuition in structure with sculptural

51   Eero Saarinen, New York Idlewild Airport
(later John F. Kennedy International Airport), 1955.

freedom in form is how undisciplined it is in individual structures and chaotic in groups.[18] Lambert and TWA share similar characteristics, but unlike TWA, the groin vaults at Lambert are rationalized to the space below, allowing for easy structural and plan expansion. This is to say, although these architectures look similar, their functional performance and the experience of the spaces are notably different.

Abbey Church, Saint Louis Priory School

The Abbey Church of the Saint Louis Priory School (1956–62), built for the Benedictine monks as part of a boys' secondary school, was one of Obata's first projects with the new firm HOK, which he formed in 1955 with George Hellmuth and George Kassabaum after the departure of Yamasaki to Detroit. Father Timothy Horner, one of the Benedictine monks who met with Obata, wanted a round church to bring the "boys much closer to the center... (so) they could pay more attention" to the services.[19] The church's structure is two rings of twenty 3-inch thin-shell concrete parabolic arches organized in a circular plan with the altar at the center (fig. 52). The structural solution is rational and sculptural, with an elegant 30-foot belfry using the same paraboloid geometry, creating a striking focal point directly above the altar (fig. 53). Pier Luigi Nervi consulted on the structure and, like Tedesko at Lambert, suggested changes that lightened the concrete shell structure. An earlier design was "a burlier, more angular concrete building."[20] His flexible approach indicates that Obata's strategy, while focused on expressing the building mass, was not dependent on it. The final plan suggests there was another equally important aim driving the tectonic solution, namely the user's experience of the space.

Although it is the structural expression of Priory Chapel most often noted by critics—*Architectural Forum* called it "the most elaborate example yet on the North American continent of a circular building in a convoluted shell form"—it is more than a "roof" building. The spatial arrangement of the altar in the center of the space surrounded by pews is unusual (fig. 54). It activates the room during services by placing the priest amid the congregation. The layout is like a theater in the round, unlike most Catholic churches or chapels where the priest performs the service at a remove. The pew arrangement brings

52   Hellmuth, Obata + Kassabaum (HOK), the Abbey
Church, Saint Louis Priory School (Priory Chapel),
Creve Coeur, Missouri, 1956–62.

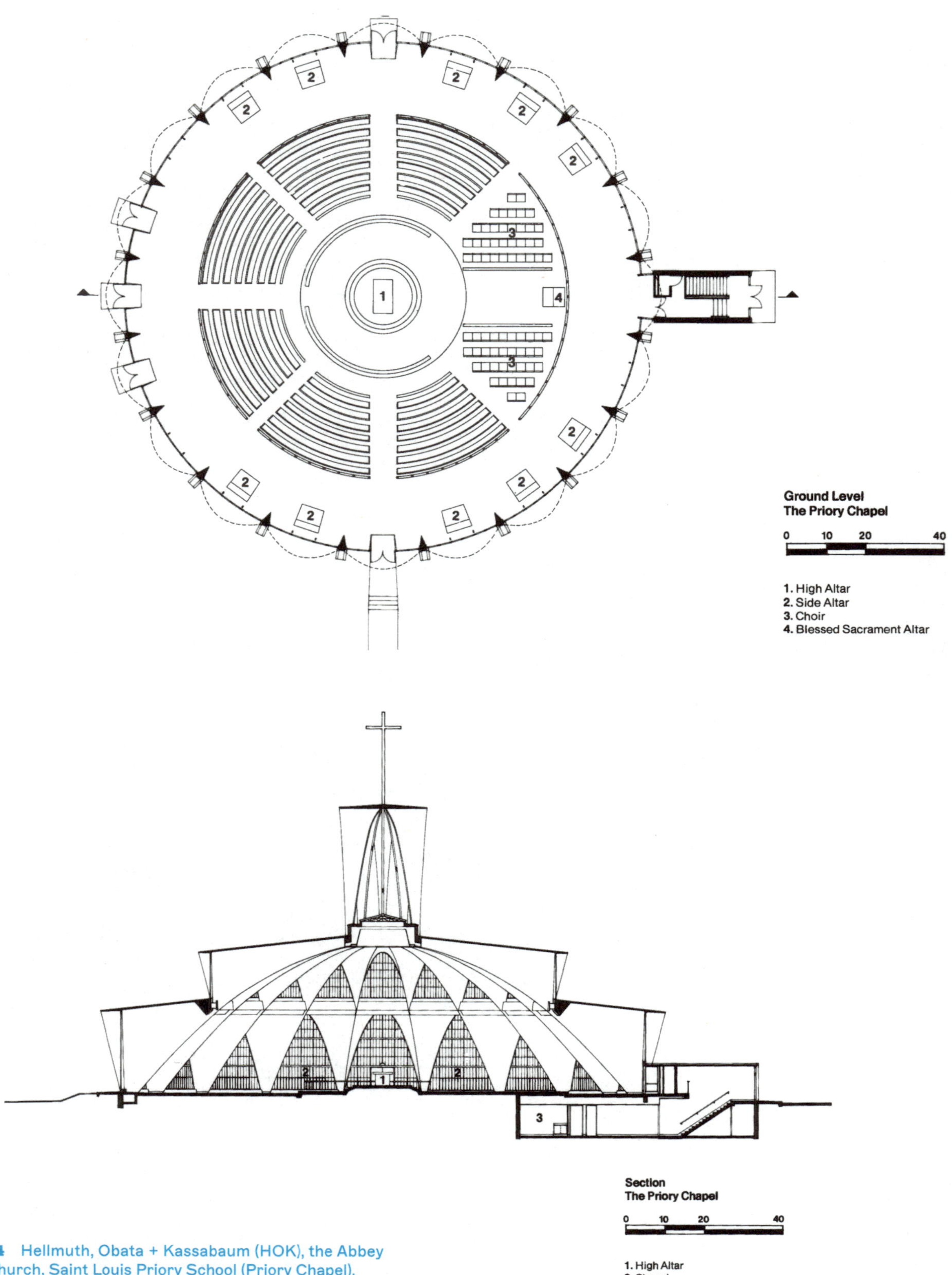

54   Hellmuth, Obata + Kassabaum (HOK), the Abbey Church, Saint Louis Priory School (Priory Chapel), Creve Coeur, Missouri, 1956–62, plan and section.

the experience of services physically and metaphorically closer to each participant. The *Kernform* of the building is this unusual expression of Father Horner's desire for spiritual intimacy with congregants, even as the *Kunstform* is the expressive geometry of the roof structure. This "both/and" approach does not negate critics' reception, but it complicates any purely modernist rational interpretation. The building is actively used to this day by the school and the parish.

James S. McDonnell Planetarium in Forest Park

The James S. McDonnell Planetarium (1963; figs. 55, 56) sits like an abstract object on the easternmost edge of Forest Park in St. Louis. At the time it was built it completed a line of earlier buildings sitting along the same ridge stretching lengthwise through the landscape. The structure is a 3-inch thin-shell concrete, 160-foot hyperbolic paraboloid floating above the landscape. Albert Alper was the structural engineer. The glass-enclosed entry is tucked under the roof shell, heightening the impression that the white form hovers above the site. The building is partially camouflaged underground. The site is artificially sloped up to the building entry located at the second floor.

Like Lambert Airport and Priory Chapel, the tendency is to read the Planetarium formally, focusing on the structural solution. Several St. Louis buildings from the same period, including Busch Stadium (1965; demolished) by Edward Durell Stone and the Buckminster Fuller–inspired Climatron (1960; see fig. 25) by Murphy and Mackey, have similar geometry. But as Obata explained, the "reason for this form was there was a planetarium inside, and . . . a stairway there wrapped around the planetarium. You could go up to the roof and from the roof, after the show, see the stars."[21] The form is sculptural but at the service of multiple spaces that operate as a folded inversion of the relationships between interior and exterior. The stairs to the exterior roof deck are outside the Planetarium auditorium but interior to the building. They take visitors from a simulation of the night sky to the actual night sky.

55 Hellmuth, Obata + Kassabaum (HOK),
James S. McDonnell Planetarium, Forest Park,
St. Louis, 1963.

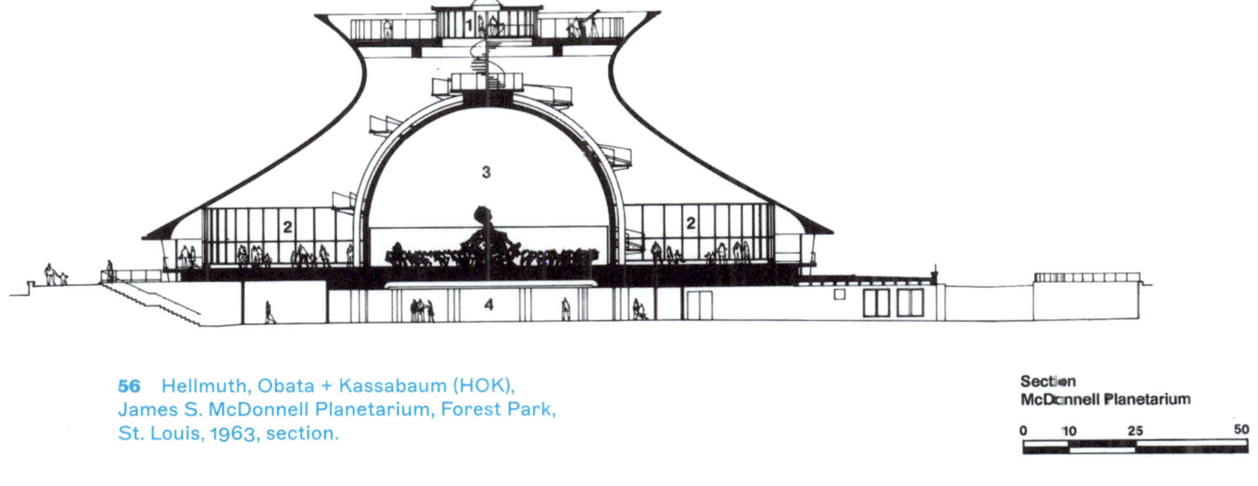

56   Hellmuth, Obata + Kassabaum (HOK),
James S. McDonnell Planetarium, Forest Park,
St. Louis, 1963, section.

Reception

All three projects' public reception was positive at the time
of their completion. Critics touted them as structurally innovative
and singular expressions of the modernist program of form
follows function. Unlike later work by both Yamasaki and Obata,
these early projects did not yet elicit overt criticism, suggesting
they were anything other than compliant with high-modernist
formalism. However, where these buildings looked like function-
alist modernism, that is, their *Kunstform*, their subtle under-
pinning of what I termed an idiosyncratic humanism led
to more ornamented and expressive buildings for Yamasaki and
buildings that bore little resemblance to the early work but
shared the same focus on the occupant's experience for Obata.
Given that most professional and critical commentary initially
focused on structural expression rather than the unusual dispo-
sition of the program sectionally and the dynamism of the
spaces, it ignored the sectional displacement of the program
elements that focused on the user experience. The experience
of moving from the great hall of the Lambert terminal to boarding, the immersion of congregants in the center of the service
in the Priory Chapel, and the intertwining of internal and
external space in the Planetarium are absent in the critique
of Obata's work. But contrary to interpretations that suggest
a discontinuity between Obata's midcentury and later work,
this focus on the communal experience of space resonates
through-out his career.

The failure of Yamasaki and Obata to continue to produce conspicuous modernist buildings in the later midcentury repositioned both as lesser figures in the modernist canon. Later criticism by figures like Paul Goldberger, writing in 1984, observed that HOK, "despite strong leadership by the conscientious and earnest Gyo Obata, has not made a major contribution to contemporary architecture." That assessment covers a lot of territory. It fails to acknowledge that critics and the public celebrated the work at midcentury.[22] But more importantly, it reveals that critics and, until recently, historians have not discerned the programmatic and often spatial continuities between their midcentury and later work. That is, they saw the *Kunstform*, but missed the *Kernform* guiding the programmatic and spatial organization of these buildings.

Wilson argued that architects like Alvar Aalto and Louis Kahn were part of the "Other Tradition," with its indeterminate formalism and humanist value accounting for the paucity of meaning when life is neglected in favor of geometric purity. Life's complexity and architecture's role in expressing it are not a problem to be rationalized or solved mechanistically as some, though not all, CIAM members advocated. Rather, Obata's approach is closer to what Häring called *Lestungform*, or the form of performance.[23] Remarking on Aalto's work, Obata echoed this idea: "Aalto broke the logic down and began to play with shape and space. The great poetry in architecture comes about in the breaking of logical rules. The question is, how to do that without jarring? It must be like Ella Fitzgerald singing—really smooth and supple."[24]

Rather than assume a certain neutrality of form, materials, function, and locale, modernism in architecture is not, as Hitchcock and Johnson argued, a transcendent International Style but one that dominated, restructured, and had authority over architecture's infinite presence, even when confronted with buildings that deny their stylistic solipsism: international as long as it's European or American; functional, but only when that means systematic or Cartesian. Wilson's other modernism offers a lens through which to see and hear architectures that look like modernist work but function in a humanist key. Gyo Obata's work is part of this other modernism.

1   Henry-Russell Hitchcock Jr. and Philip Johnson, *The International Style: Architecture since 1922* (New York: W. W. Norton, 1932). The exhibition made a three-year tour of the US. Four out of the ten projects featured American architects.

2   Colin St John Wilson, *The Other Tradition of Modern Architecture* (London: Academy Editions, 1995), 13–17.

3   Häring articulated this position throughout his career. See *Wege zur Form* (1925), https://doi.org/10.11588/diglit.13211.3; and "Probleme des Bauens," *Der Neubau* 17, Peter Blundell-Jones (trans.), September 10, 1924. See also St John Wilson, *The Other Tradition*, 18.

4   See for example "Hellmuth, Obata and Kassabaum, Master Architects," *Kenosha News* (Kenosha, WI), January 27, 1970, accessed September 6, 2023, https://www.newspapers.com/image/597448051; Jack Grone, "Obata Still Devotes 80% of His Time to Design Work," *St. Louis Business Journal* 11, no. 31, April 22, 1991.

5   For more on Obata and HOK, see Patrick MacLeamy, *Designing a World-Class Architecture Firm: The People, Stories, and Strategies Behind HOK* (Hoboken, NJ: Wiley, 2020); and Eric Mumford, ed., *Modern Architecture in St. Louis: Washington University and Postwar American Architecture, 1948–1973* (St. Louis: Washington University School of Architecture, 2004).

6   Eliel Saarinen, *The City: Its Growth, Its Decay, Its Future* (New York: Reinhold, 1943).

7   Gyo Obata, "St. Louis, A Study in Urban Decay" (master's thesis, Cranbrook Academy of Art, 1945), 6–7, https://openscholarship.wustl.edu/books/55/.

8   Eileen Gray and Jean Badovici, "From Eclecticism to Doubt," *L'Architecture vivante* (Autumn and Winter, 1929): 20.

9   Obata, "St. Louis, A Study in Urban Decay," 67.

10   Ibid., 62.

11   Bötticher applied the terms in the eighteenth century to separate static structure from artistic appliqué. Karl Bötticher, *Die Tektonik der Hellenen*, 2 vols. (Berlin: Ernst & Korn, 1871–1881).

12   Dale Allen Gyure, *Minoru Yamasaki: Humanist Architecture for a Modernist World* (New Haven, CT: Yale University Press, 2017), 31–32.

13   Anton Tedesko, the engineer at that time working most commonly with thin-shelled concrete, contributed to the realization of the groin vaults.

14   Jeremy Kargon uses the term for religious architecture, but it is equally appropriate for large-scale civic works such as auditoriums, planetariums, and airports. See Jeremy Kargon, "Seeing, Not Knowing: Symbolism, Art, and 'Opticalism' in Mid-Century American Religious Architecture" in *Modernism and American Mid-20th Century Sacred Architecture*, ed. Anat Geva (London: Routledge, 2018), 235–54.

15   "New Thinking on Airport Terminals," *Architectural Forum* 97 (November 1952), 130–43.

16   Dale Allen Gyure notes that Yamasaki's designs were not sectionally active: "He was no spatial innovator. Throughout his career his building demonstrated a consistent absence of spatial variety." Gyure, *Minoru Yamasaki*, 257.

17   Thomas H. Creighton, "The New Sensualism II," *Progressive Architecture* (October 1959): 180–87.

18   Ibid., 187.

19   Gyo Obata, "Adaptive Reuse of the American Zinc Building and Other Works" (talk), Mid-Century Modern Structures: Materials and Preservation Symposium, April 14–16, 2015, St. Louis, Missouri, accessed August 25, 2023, https://www.nps.gov/articles/000/adaptive-reuse-of-the-american-zinc-building-and-other-works.htm.

20   Walter McQuade, *Architecture in the Real World: The Work of HOK*, (New York: H. N. Abrams, 1984), 16.

21   Obata, "Acaptive Reuse."

22   Several midcentury projects by Obata and HOK were on the covers of *Time*, *Life*, and *Progressive Architecture*.

23   Peter Blundell-Jones, *Hugo Häring: The Organic Versus the Geometric* (Stuttgart: Edition Axel Menges, 1999), 92.

24   McQuade, *Architecture in the Real World*, 2.

The Architecture of Charles E. Fleming

Shantel Blakely

If the critical assessment of an architect and his projects is mainly concerned with a building's formal logic or self-consistency, assessing the work of Charles E. Fleming (b. 1937), an African American architect who built mainly for the Black community in late-twentieth-century St. Louis, is a challenging exercise. Fleming's community was subject at the time to racial segregation and its geographic effects, and this raises questions about what that situation demanded of him and what it meant for his architecture. But if a focus on form alone in Fleming's projects would risk overlooking what their social context may have contributed, there is also a danger in overemphasizing this context, for if a modern functional building could be meaningful just by being built for Blacks in a certain place and time, there would be no scope for achievement, no material for critical reflection. What work would be left for form or tangible qualities to do?

In fact, both Fleming's biography and works suggest that even in Jim Crow–era St. Louis, conditions were not as bleak as a present-day reader might expect. Blacks lived in an archipelago of isolated settlements, often in rented homes or multifamily housing near industrial sites or rail lines. Some of their neighborhoods had no commercial buildings at all. Many of their buildings were decades old, built on the cheap, or inherited from another demographic such as German immigrants. New architecture was being built in St. Louis but normally in "whites-only" spaces. The built environment visually signaled the marginal status of the Black community and projected the stereotype of its powerlessness and narrow scope of life. Within their communities, however, Blacks were gaining mobility and freedom during this period. The pages of Black newspapers such as the *St. Louis Argus* and *St. Louis American* during the 1950s and 1960s give the impression of a community that not only kept track of events but also found achievements in education, service, business, and the arts to celebrate.[1] Most members of the Black community had come to the city from the South after the end of slavery; they had sought work and security and embraced commonly held American ideals of material prosperity. This community knew that appearances were powerful; Fleming's early work shows that it was not unheard of, even if it was still rare, for a family or group to commission an architectural work in the 1960s.

Early Influences

Charles E. Fleming was born in a part of St. Louis County where Maplewood, Clayton, and Richmond Heights converged. His mother had been born there too; her parents as well as Fleming's father were part of the Great Migration in which Blacks left the South for northern industrial towns. Fleming's father hailed from a Mississippi town where a Black man might face death from a single misplaced word; he maintained all his life a habit of silence. Fleming too would come to be known as a man of few words, but as a child he showed a talent for decoration that was encouraged by his teachers and relatives.[2]

Growing up, Fleming spent most of his time in his grandparents' neighborhood. Some of their neighbors had high-status service jobs in nearby white households; others provided unskilled labor to a nearby brick manufactory or lumberyard. Still others, like Fleming's grandfather Thomas Gaskin, worked in building trades. It was common practice to do small jobs for cash or barter in this family-centered enclave; the architect Michael E. Willis, who briefly lived there, recalls that his parents and their neighbors were always working.[3] From his grandfather Gaskin, a sought-after tradesman who specialized in house painting, wallpapering, and minor construction, Fleming learned the sizes of nails and wood pieces at a young age from being sent to the lumberyard or hardware store.[4]

As a teenager, working beside his grandfather in Richmond Heights to move houses out of the way of what is now the Interstate 64 extension, Fleming caught the eye of the local building commissioner Ed Kelly and a group of younger architects. From these men he learned about the Building Certificate program in University College at Washington University; he enrolled in 1955. His instructors, including Professor Roland W. Bockhorst and the recent graduate Edward J. Thias, were drawn from the University's architecture school. Washington University was legally desegregated in the mid-1940s following action by the NAACP, but Fleming recalls a remark here and there from a professor who seemed never to have taught a Black student. One instructor noticed Fleming's well-developed biceps and said half-joking that he "should have been a fighter." Fleming also recalls that his skills surprised everyone and that his classmates accepted him; "We were as brothers in arms."[5]

In school and at work, Fleming learned to make sun-and-shadow studies of his designs and to design for construction in wood, concrete block, and brick. He grew familiar with the standard ranch house and commercial building. His early designs resemble the work of his instructor Thias. Thias in turn would recall years later, in a self-published autobiography, the influence of the Swiss architect Alfred Roth, who was a visiting faculty member at Washington University around 1950. Roth was widely known for his book *The New Architecture* (1940), a compendium of modern buildings in European towns in the 1930s, and for his membership in CIAM, the International Congresses of Modern Architecture. The modernism advocated by Roth employed a visual language of simple rectangular volumes and abundant illumination through large windows, consistent with his experience working for Le Corbusier and his involvement in the 1927 Weissenhofsiedlung (Weissenhof working-class housing complex) in Stuttgart; but as Thias observed with approval, Roth made a priority of meeting needs rather than expressing an individual style.[6]

Early Works

Fleming's architecture, like Alfred Roth's, put function and construction before individual expression. There are trademark motifs in his buildings, such as the "U"- or "C"-shaped windows on the St. Louis Comprehensive Neighborhood Health Center (1974; see fig. 26), the State Community College in East St. Louis (1977), and the renovated building at 3531 Lindell Boulevard that housed his office for several years (fig. 61). But his commercial buildings, like the unadorned rectangular volume of the Wade Funeral Home on Natural Bridge Road (1965, demolished), recall the designs of Thias and his contemporaries: flat-roofed, single-storied buildings with structures of steel or wood framing and non-load-bearing masonry walls broken at intervals by strips or grids of windows.[7]

57 Charles E. Fleming, Leslie Bond residence, St. Louis, 1962.

Fleming used a variant of this contemporary style in his projects for Black clients in St. Louis. A 1962 house at 5583 Lindell Boulevard resembles a pair of boxes with double-hipped roofs, including a detached garage connected by a breezeway (fig. 57). The design defies the revivalist status quo embodied in the imitation Tudor and Cape Cod homes that line the boulevard, which borders Forest Park's northern edge. Fleming's clients, Dr. Leslie Bond and family, were part of a social change too: at a moment when housing discrimination against Blacks and Jews was still widespread in St. Louis, the Bonds became the first Blacks to own a home on Lindell.[8] For St. Philip's Lutheran Church (1965) Fleming used a masonry-and-vertical-windows design to propose a novel monumentality for this structure in the Ville, one of the main commercial centers of Black St. Louis, not far from Homer G. Phillips Hospital, the first teaching hospital for Blacks west of the Mississippi and the only public hospital for Blacks in St. Louis (see fig. 8). The church stood in contrast to the style of that prestigious institution, which was designed by city architect Albert Osburg with Georgian-style details, constructed in the mid-1930s. In another design from 1965, Mt. Esther Baptist Church (since altered), Fleming strategically placed subtly decorative elements to present the box-like building as a house of worship (fig. 58). It was not monumental;

58   Charles E. Fleming, Mt. Esther Baptist Church, St. Louis, 1965.

it faced the street with a facade of similar height and width to the houses around it on Greer Avenue. Fleming added a slender steel cross, a small loggia in a porch at the corner entrance, and a low wall around the front yard that formed an enclosure where the congregation could gather informally.[9]

Some doors would remain closed to Fleming in the professional world. One local firm of consulting engineers would not work with him, as they did with his white contemporaries, so he learned to compile his own structural and mechanical drawings to be stamped by individual engineers.[10] But Fleming had entered the profession of architecture at the beginning of a period of opportunity for Blacks in St. Louis and across the United States. The Supreme Court had struck down legal segregation with Brown v. Board of Education in 1954, Fleming's junior year in high school, and while segregation would persist in St. Louis in the 1960s, Blacks were gaining access to higher education in greater numbers and entering professions such as architecture, as indicated by the founding of NOMA, the National Organization of Minority Architects, in 1971.[11] Just a generation earlier a factory job, a position in service in a wealthy family home, or working as a security guard or railway porter had been considered a "good" job.[12]

Fleming also benefited from President Lyndon B. Johnson's War on Poverty, which introduced a slew of programs and opportunities beginning in 1964. Certain projects initiated by St. Louis Mayor Alfonso J. Cervantes (in office 1965–73), including the construction of medical clinics and other facilities, were sup-ported in part by funds from the federal departments of Housing and Urban Development and Health and Human Services.[13] Such programs would end after Johnson's exit from the White House in 1969, but at least three of Fleming's 1970s projects—the Carr Central Community Center (1974), Courtney Health Care Center (1975; fig. 59), and Arthur J. Kennedy Skill Training Center (1975)—were built with the support of these federal programs.

In 1968 Fleming entered a partnership with Carey K. Jenkins and began work on the Dr. Martin Luther King Jr. Community Hospital in the Watts neighborhood of Los Angeles.[14] Jenkins would remain in Los Angeles while Fleming, as head of the St. Louis office, oversaw such projects as the renovation of and new entrance for Homer G. Phillips Hospital (c. 1975; fig. 60).

59 Charles E. Fleming, Courtney Health
Care Center, St. Louis, 1975.

60 Charles E. Fleming, left, with Carey K. Jenkins
in front of their renovated entrance to Homer
G. Phillips Hospital, St. Louis, photograph mid-1970s.

61   Charles E. Fleming, St. Louis office
of Jenkins-Fleming Inc., early 1970s.

Jenkins-Fleming Inc. undertook projects with large corporate firms as well. With Walter A. Netsch of Skidmore, Owings & Merrill, they tried to save the Pruitt-Igoe apartment complex (1970),[15] and with Hellmuth, Obata + Kassabaum they helped design the Alfonso J. Cervantes Convention and Exhibition Center in downtown St. Louis (1976). Fleming also joined local commissions and task forces; with six other professionals and scholars he was part of the Urban Housing Foundation, which advised inner-city communities on the development and preservation of housing.[16] After a decade of collaboration, Fleming parted ways with Jenkins and entered a new phase with Fleming Corporation. By the mid-1980s, and until he ceased to practice in the early 2000s, he sustained this office with major service contracts as well as private projects.

A Forward-Looking Approach

A careful look at Fleming's projects reveals the various ways his work reflects the confluence of the early influence of both the construction practices of his grandfather and others in their neighborhood and the late-modern architectural style of his instructors at Washington University. The aesthetic character of the buildings he designed proposes an optimistic and forward-looking tone; these projects often marked an achievement or an advance in the access of Black St. Louis residents to a higher level of visibility or participation in the public sphere.

62   Original location of Thomas E. Rusan's medical practice in 1940s–50s, North Webster, Missouri.

One notable example is Fleming's clinic for Thomas E. Rusan (1959; demolished), a Black doctor in North Webster, a historically all-Black section of the St. Louis suburb Webster Groves. The clinic, which grew from an abandoned filling station, was a modern replacement for the large house, a few blocks away, where Rusan had practiced for more than a decade (fig. 62).[17] Most documentation of the project is gone—there is even less for Fleming's 1965 clinic for another physician, Dr. Hoard, which was built in Kinloch—but as shown in a photograph clipped by Fleming's mother from a local paper in 1959, Rusan's clinic was a single-story, flat-roofed box, entered through a sheltered porch behind a screen made of perforated concrete block (fig. 63).[18] It resembles the "medical center" scheme shown in undated drawings in a collection of Fleming's student work.[19] The newspaper reported that the air-conditioned, state-of-the art facility had its own laboratory and X-ray machines and that over five hundred people attended its opening celebration, including Webster Groves's mayor.

A second notable project, Gateway Bank (1965), was commissioned by a group of local Black businessmen. The mistreatment of Black patrons at banks was routine under segregation and gained notoriety in the early 1960s when Blacks were rarely employed as tellers, even at branches in their own neighborhoods. In August 1963 a picket line was formed and sit-ins were led by the St. Louis chapter of the Congress of Racial Equality (CORE) (fig. 64).[20] This led the group of Black businessmen to conceive Gateway Bank (fig. 65).[21] The site was a cube-shaped former union hall in a wide lot at 3412 North Union Boulevard. To research the required equipment Fleming visited two banks in Kansas City, Missouri—Douglass Bank (est. 1947) and Swope Parkway Bank (est. 1961), both of which were part of a wave of Black-owned bank openings that began in the South.[22] To turn the ex–union hall into a bank, Fleming had drive-in windows installed on one side and hung a series of evenly spaced, tapered concrete strips on the facade, each extending from the first floor to the parapet. These elements' fin-like shape calls to mind the Optimist International building (1961) by Schwarz and Van Hoefen in St. Louis's Central West End; in another allusion to the city, a sign in the bank's parking lot reproduced in miniature the parabola of Eero Saarinen's Gateway Arch, which was under construction at the time. Inside were the usual consulting tables and seating and a long counter for tellers. Customers were exhilarated to feel welcome in a commercial bank.[23]

Fleming's Parks Chapel AME (African Methodist Episcopal) Church (1969; fig. 66) is a striking example of the community-specific resonance in certain of his projects. The new building marked a milestone for its congregation, which had existed in North Webster for fifty years at the time of the commission. The neighborhood had grown as newly arrived migrants joined a small settlement of formerly enslaved persons. From the 1940s

63 Charles E. Fleming, Rusan Medical Clinic, North Webster, Missouri, 1953, newspaper article.

64 CORE (Congress of Racial Equality) members protest the discriminatory hiring practices of regional banks, St. Louis, 1963.

to the mid-1950s, the area was home to Fleming's high school, Douglass, the only high school for Blacks in St. Louis County. North Webster was also known for its churches—so numerous at one point that residents would later recall falling asleep to church music—but while some congregations could afford a purpose-built building after years of weekly collections, others never had a building of their own.[24]

65   Charles E. Fleming, Gateway Bank under construction, St. Louis, 1965.

Fleming's design for the chapel was a one-story rectangular volume set on a grassy plinth along Ravine Avenue, visible from the local main thoroughfare, Brentwood Boulevard, a few blocks away. The building had a space for gathering near the sheltered entrance, reached by a short flight of steps. At the opposite end, behind the altar, was another protruding central bay with a single stained-glass window, probably by the Emil Frei studio. The roof, made of inverted wooden trusses whose peaks point downward, is flat as seen from outside but gives a convex ceiling to the large rectangular sanctuary within.

66   Charles E. Fleming, Parks Chapel AME (African Methodist Episcopal) Church, Webster Groves, Missouri, 1969.

With its boxy shape, flat roof, and prominent brick and land-scaping, this church illustrates the stylistic hybridity in Fleming's work. The rectangular main volume and limited decorative elements are in keeping with the unadorned form of modernist buildings, but the prominence of bricks and site work highlights the fact that Fleming could design with confidence with masonry and landscaping, which were specialties of local Black tradesmen. One expression of this pairing is an unusual detail: at the top of the front wall and on the sills of its five narrow win-dows, a course of bricks is set at an angle, which casts a line of shadow. More importantly, the tilted course allows the facade to shed water without the need of any other material such as stone or copper. This efficient way of meeting architectural requirements shows how Fleming could mediate between mod-ern aesthetics and the constraints of a given project. Parks Chapel was not imitated by later neighborhood buildings, but its distinctive form added to a lively eclecticism in a neighborhood with "shotgun" houses, concrete block homes made from kits, and Lustron porcelain enameled steel homes, as well as older church buildings such as Nazarene Baptist Church (1924), with its unusual triple-gabled facade.[25]

Arthur J. Kennedy Skill Training Center

For the Arthur J. Kennedy Skill Training Center (1975; demolished), Fleming's client was the St. Louis Model City Agency, an office in City Hall that was dedicated to the federally funded program.

The Skill Training Center was an experimental vocational training school that gave selected inner-city high school graduates a path to union jobs by providing trade education and job placement at no cost to the student. Its mastermind, the businessman and influential civic figure Arthur J. Kennedy Sr., was a Tuskegee Institute graduate who ran a local sheet metal company. Kennedy was passionate about labor issues; as a leading NAACP member in the early 1960s, for example, he had fought successfully to desegregate Ranken Technical Academy, St. Louis's preeminent trade school.[26] Kennedy led the Center's development as head of the Model City Agency, a position to which he was appointed by Mayor Cervantes in 1969. In recognition of his influence, the building was named after him in a dedication ceremony in 1976.[27]

The Center's main funding source, the Model Cities program in the federal government's Department of Housing and Urban Development, was part of a campaign in President Lyndon B. Johnson's War on Poverty that promoted the application of holistic, systems-thinking methods to public health problems in cities. The Center's operation involved several city departments and the Board of Education; its funding would also come in part from the Manpower program in the Department of Labor.[28]

The program of Fleming's building was complex, for it was essentially a school, office building, and industrial workplace all in one. It was constructed on a limited budget and built on a former industrial site at the corner of North Market Street and Leffingwell Street, not far from the vacated Pruitt-Igoe complex. The few photographs in Fleming's archive show a composition dominated by the exterior walls of the workshops, which appear as different-sized volumes. The building was lauded for its expression of adequacy, solidity, and performance. The critic George McCue, who included the Skill Training Center in his guidebook *The Building Art in St. Louis,* recognized the clarity of the building design; he remarked that its "internal subdivisions are expressed in wall projections and setbacks."[29] The standing-seam metal roof was turned down to cover the

upper portion of the facades. Between roof and walls was a con-
tinuous strip of sloped translucent panels that let ample light
into the workshops, all but eliminating the need for conventional
windows. The exterior walls were made of freestanding
reinforced concrete block. Fleming kept the steel roof system
exposed on the inside, to show the students how it worked.[30]
Inside, the building had wide hallways with painted cinderblock
walls and linoleum floors. There was a long counter for student
services and a clerical instruction room with rows of typewrit-
ers under a dropped ceiling with fluorescent lights. In the
workspaces students could practice on heavy machinery such
as winches, presses, saws, and car maintenance equipment;
building maintenance students could build full-scale, wood-frame
walls.[31] Fleming endowed the spaces around the building with
thoughtful details that invited a sense of ownership. For example,
he placed a patio with beds of grass along North Market Street
and masonry planters on both sides of the entrance, with knee-
high walls suitable for sitting on.

67 Opening of the Arthur J. Kennedy Skill Training Center,
with Kennedy flanked by Mayor John Poelker (left) and A. J.
Wilson, St. Louis, 1975.

By 1975, when the Skill Training Center opened (fig. 67), Johnson's term in office was long over and the Model Cities initiative had ended. City Hall sustained the Center until 1984. When the program closed amid scarce funding and too few qualified students in St. Louis due to population decline, the building was abandoned.[32] Nevertheless, its significance remained. In 1996, when it was slated for demolition, an alderwoman and a local activist camped out in front of it to protest what they saw as the city's abandonment of inner-city communities.[33] That penultimate episode in the building's life, before it was razed, indicates how, in its brief life, the building had become a potent symbol of government investment in community well-being. It is telling that even in ruins, when the building's metal roof panels were gone and the interiors exposed, the sign out front with the school's name spelled out in capital letters remained intact.[34]

A Suburban Home

Fleming's move to the suburbs in 1970 followed a national pattern that began in the 1950s, in which middle-class families of all races left the inner city. In the house that he designed for himself and his wife in Town and Country, a St. Louis suburb, he adopted a distinctly non-urban attitude by working in wood in contrast to the masonry emphasis of his city buildings. Fleming never admitted to any influence, but the house itself (figs. 68–71), with its group of sheds clad in vertical wooden siding, suggests an affinity for the rustic modernism exemplified in Rush House at Sea Ranch by Charles W. Moore and William Turnbull (1970). The components of a 1980 renovation, which included a swimming pool enclosed by a tall hedge and a studio above the garage, seemingly nestled in the foliage, would heighten the house's pastoral atmosphere.

The Legacy of Charles E. Fleming

In conditions of scarcity, all architecture tends toward the symbolic; but there is more to Fleming's projects than just the impact of their existence. His buildings brought a new visibility and legibility to Black spaces in the built environment of mid-century St. Louis. The lingering framework of segregation is a key part of the context in which these projects resonate, but as discussed, the architect's decisions and details were crucial in bringing the buildings to life as bearers of messages. The intersection of Fleming's professional identity with his

68   Charles E. Fleming, Fleming residence,
Town and Country, Missouri, 1970–80, entrance.

69   Charles E. Fleming, Fleming residence,
Town and Country, Missouri, 1970–80, greenhouse.

71   Charles E. Fleming, Fleming residence,
Town and Country, Missouri, 1970–80, rear courtyard.

70   Charles E. Fleming, Fleming residence,
Town and Country, Missouri, 1970–80,
office and walkway over pool.

close connection to the Black community was essential: without the loyalty to St. Louis's Black community that Fleming maintained all his life, no architect would have taken an interest in some of the projects described above, nor in other important works not mentioned here, such as his series of renovations to city parks in the 1980s. Without his formation as an educated, licensed architect, Fleming would not have been able to produce buildings whose sophistication was comparable to other new buildings across the city; yet the salience of his work as interventions in the physical and social fabric of St. Louis owes something to that parity.

The situation of midcentury St. Louis meant that in Fleming's projects a building's formal and tangible qualities could not be freely chosen; they were subject to locally determined material and technical constraints. The necessity of working in brick, for instance, would have put in question any architect's capacity to produce a modern aesthetic, which is associated with smooth monochrome walls and expansive windows. The recognizably modern character of Fleming's buildings, including his brick buildings, speaks to his ability to overcome that challenge. His works draw meaning not only from their architectural design, or from how they met the needs of their clients and community, but also from the expression of relationships between each design and its cultural-historical moment or place of construction. His projects spoke *in* a certain time, as well as *of* a certain time and *to* it, through both their form and their very being.

Research and documentation for this essay was supported by the Getty Research Institute, the Graham Foundation for Advanced Research in the Visual Arts, and faculty research grants from Washington University in St. Louis and Rice University. Special thanks to Melvin L. Mitchell, Michael E. Willis, and Michael Anderson, architects, for sharing their stories; archivist Charles E. Brown at the St. Louis Mercantile Library for research guidance; archivists Molly Kodner at the Missouri Historical Society library and Miranda Rectenwald at Washington University Libraries Special Collections; Robin D. G. Kelley, Gary B. Nash Professor of American History at the University of California, Los Angeles, for his encouragement; and Eric P. Mumford, Rebecca and John Voyles Professor of Architecture at Washington University, for my introduction to the architect.

Charles E. Fleming passed away in summer 2024 as this publication was going to press. This essay could not have been written without our many conversations in which he revisited episodes of his life and shared his detailed recollections of projects and people. Getting to know this intelligent, reticent, resilient person, and enjoying his wry sense of humor, enlarged my understanding of what it means to be an architect and to be human. I hope that by way of this essay, and through the local archives Fleming helped create, others will learn from him too.

1 The *St. Louis Argus* and *St. Louis American* are available on microfilm at the Missouri Historical Society.

2 Melvin Mitchell, interview with the author, November 2022; Charles E. Fleming, interview with the author. The architect Mitchell was an employee of Fleming in the 1970s.

3 Michael E. Willis, panel discussion, "African American Architecture in St. Louis: The Case of Charles E. Fleming," Mildred Lane Kemper Art Museum, January 30, 2021, https://youtu.be /JB2ILw3CHI0?feature=shared.

4 Charles E. Fleming, interview with the author, July 2021; "The Fleming Family," *Proud* 7, no. 3 (1977): 24.

5 Fleming, interview with the author, July 2021. On the integration of Washington University in St. Louis, see Ralph E. Morrow, *Washington University in St. Louis: A History* (St. Louis: Missouri Historical Society, 1996), 463–71; Candace O'Connor, *Beginning a Great Work: Washington University in St. Louis, 1853–2003* (St. Louis: Washington University in St. Louis, 2003).

6 Thias reports that Roth was a visiting design critic in 1950 and 1951. Alfred Roth, "Architectural Education," *Architects' Year Book* 2 (1947): 115–20. Excerpted in Edward J. Thias, *Architectural Work of Edward J. Thias, Architect: Functional Architecture*, unpublished manuscripts, c. 1980–1990s. Edward J. Thias Papers (S0742), State Historical Society of Missouri Research Center–St. Louis.

7 See for example Thias's station building for Southwestern Bell. *Architectural Work of Edward J. Thias, Architect*, Edward J. Thias Papers.

8 Sandra Jordan, "Dr. Leslie F. Bond Sr. Passes at 85," *St. Louis American*, March 28, 2013, https://www.stlamerican .com/news/local_news/dr-leslie-f-bond -sr-passes-at-85/article_ed29cdb6-9734 -11e2-9d00-001a4bcf887a.html.

9 Photographs of these projects are held in the Charles E. Fleming Archive, Missouri Historical Society Library and Research Center, St. Louis.

10 Charles E. Fleming, interview with the author, December 2023; Richard ("Rod") Henmi, "Taking Down the Walls," *St. Louis Post-Dispatch*, August 4, 1994.

11 See "History," NOMA (website), https://www.noma.net/history.

12 Fleming, interview with the author, December 2023.

13 M-151: St. Louis Model Cities Association Archive, Special Collections of the St. Louis Mercantile Library at the University of Missouri–St. Louis.

14 Jenkins-Fleming Inc. designed a physicians' dormitory. "Watts Finally Gets a Hospital," *Ebony* 30, no. 2 (December 1974): 124–34.

15 See "Pruitt-Igoe Demolition to Start," *St. Louis Post-Dispatch*, January 17, 1972; and "6 Firms to Offer Center Designs," *St. Louis Post-Dispatch*, January 9, 1973.

16 "Free Help to Community Groups Offered by Housing Foundation," *St. Louis Post-Dispatch*, February 24, 1966.

17 Louis Davis et al., "A Black Community of Faith and Hope: North Webster Historic Walking Tour," pamphlet published by the Webster Groves Historical Society, 2017, https:// historicwebster.org/wp-content /uploads/2019/09/A-Black-Community -of-Faith-and-Hope-North-Webster -Walking-Tour-min.pdf, 12.

18 The details of the project and dedication were reported in a local newspaper, source and author unknown; the clipping is in Fleming's personal papers.

19 "Charles Fleming Student Work," Department of Special Collections, Washington University Libraries, LH2021-013-003, LH2021-013-004.

20 "CORE Members Protest Jefferson Bank and Trust," *St. Louis Globe-Democrat*, October 10, 1963.

21 "The History," St. Louis Community Credit Union (website), https:// gatewayslccu.com. A model for Gateway Bank may have been the New Age Federal Savings and Loan Association, which was founded by a group of Black businessmen in 1915 and moved in 1958 into its own purpose-built building at 1401 North Kingshighway, now St. Louis City Landmark #127. See https://www .stlouis-mo.gov/government /departments/planning/cultural -resources/city-landmarks/new-age -federal-savings-and-loan.cfm.

22 Charles E. Fleming, interview with the author, December 2020.

23 Linda Lockhart, "Norman Seay Looks Back on Jefferson Bank and Local Struggle for Civil Rights," St. Louis Public Radio, August 24, 2010, first published in the *St. Louis Beacon*, https://www.stlpr.org/government -politics-issues/2010-08-24/norman -seay-looks-back-on-jefferson-bank -and-local-struggle-for-civil-rights; see also Dale Singer, "Many Remember Gateway Bank as a Milestone in Local Civil Rights History," St. Louis Public Radio, November 9, 2009, first published in the *St. Louis Beacon*, https://www.stlpr.org/economy -business/2009-11-09/many-remember -gateway-bank-as-milestone-in-local -civil-rights-history.

24 Davis, "A Black Community," 7.

25 Ibid.

26 "Ranken School Ends Its Ban on Negro Students," *St. Louis Post-Dispatch*, February 22, 1963.

27 Among those participating in the ceremony were John B. Ervin, dean of the School of Continuing Education at Washington University, and city representatives. "Training Center Dedication Program," *St. Louis Globe Democrat*, October 12, 1976, St. Louis Mercantile Library at the University of Missouri–St. Louis.

28 Alexander Von Hoffmann, "Into the Wild Blue Yonder: The Urban Crisis, Rocket Science, and the Pursuit of Transformation Housing Policy in the Great Society, Part Two." Working Paper, Joint Center for Housing Studies, Harvard University, March 2011, https:// www.jchs.harvard edu/sites/default/files /media/imp/w11-3_von_hoffman.pdf. See also "Training Center Dedication Program," *St. Louis Post-Dispatch*, October 10, 1976.

29 George McCue, *The Building Art in St. Louis: Two Centuries* (1967), 3rd ed (St. Louis: American Institute of Architects, 1981), 116.

30 Charles E. Fleming, interview with the author, October 2022.

31 Photographs by Robert LaRouche, *St. Louis Post-Dispatch*, June 25, 1984; Charles E. Fleming Archive, Missouri Historical Society.

32 Staci D. Kramer, "North Side Skill Center to Close its Doors," *St. Louis Post-Dispatch*, June 25, 1984; see also Staci D. Kramer, "12 Kennedy Center Graduates Are Last, But Not Least," *St. Louis Post-Dispatch*, June 25, 1984.

33 Carolyn Tuft, "Camp Out; Alderman, Activist Protest Plan to Demolish Center," *St. Louis Post-Dispatch*, October 11, 1996.

34 Photograph by Kevin Manning, in ibid.

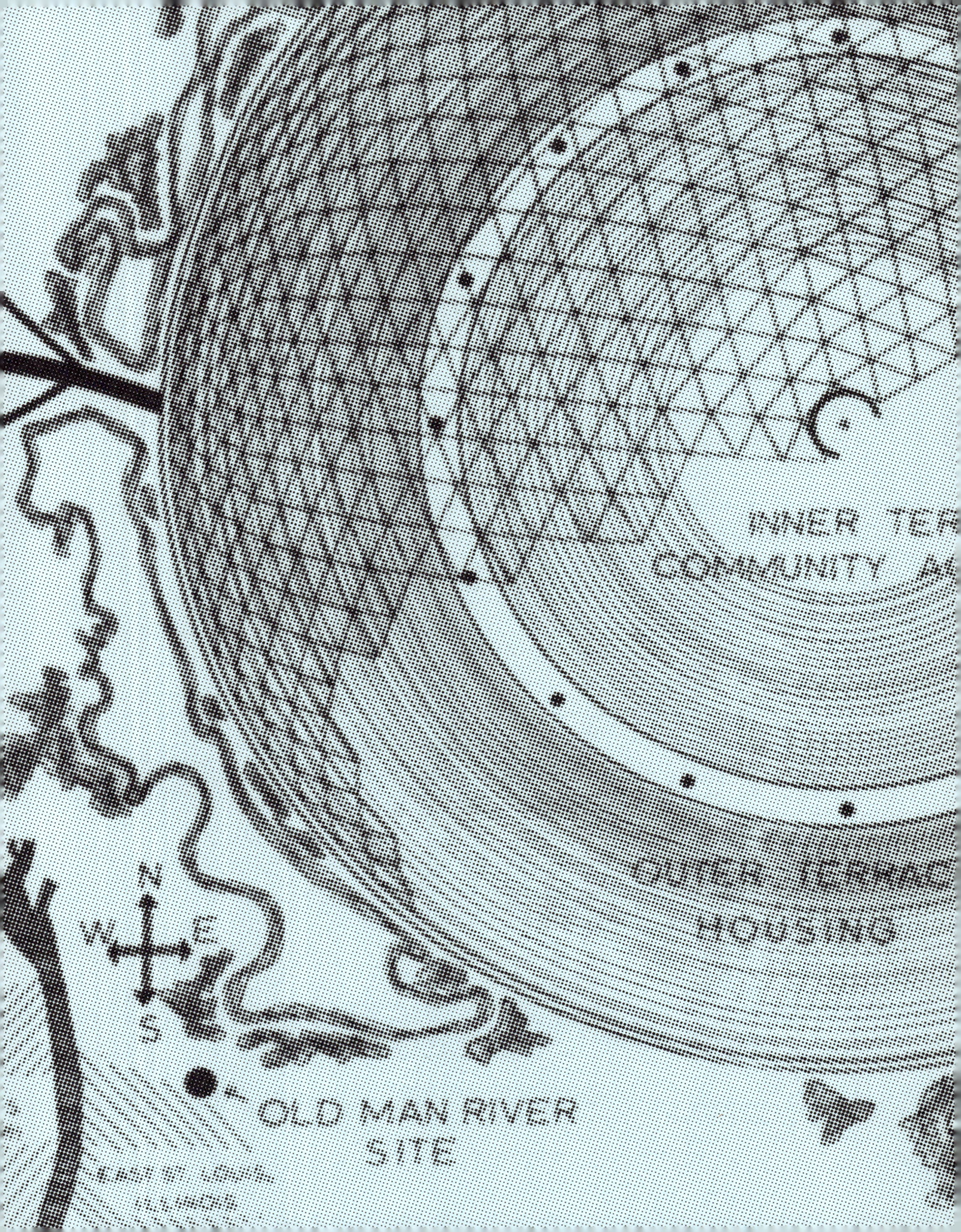

INNER TER
COMUNITY A
OUTER TER
HOUSING
N
W E
S
OLD MAN RIVER
SITE

Buckminster Fuller's Old Man River's City: A Visionary City Unrealized

John C. Guenther, FAIA, LEED AP

In 1970 the architect, engineer, teacher, cartographer, philosopher, scientist, writer, lecturer, futurist, visionary, inventor, and designer Buckminster Fuller (1895–1983) was asked by his friend Katherine Dunham, the internationally influential African American dancer, choreographer, author, educator, anthropologist, and social activist, to design an urban housing development in East St. Louis, Illinois, that would solve the problem of the city's lack of low-cost, affordable housing. This resulted in Old Man River's City, Fuller's design concept for a massive new urban structure to house 125,000 people in a one-mile diameter "moon crater" 50 stories and 500 feet in height. The design included terraced housing facing outward and community functions facing inward, all under a quarter-sphere geodesic "umbrella" dome, supported 500 feet above the earth and rising to a height of 1,000 feet.

Fuller and His Designs for the St. Louis Region, 1954–1973

Fuller's search for the "coordinate system of nature" led him to develop and popularize the geodesic dome concept; he has recently been described as the "inventor of the future."[1] The St. Louis region has one of the greatest concentrations of Fuller-designed dome structures—temporary, permanent, and unbuilt. In 1954 architecture students at Washington University in St. Louis built a temporary geodesic dome of his design (fig. 72). The 1956 Mid-America Jubilee celebrated St. Louis and its fashion industries and featured a temporary, Fuller-designed geodesic dome on the St. Louis riverfront. In 1960 Fuller had a geodesic dome home built for himself and his wife, Anne Hewlett Fuller, in Carbondale, Illinois, where he was a professor in the Department of Design at Southern Illinois University (SIU).[2] The Missouri Botanical Garden Climatron (1960) was based on the design theory and patent application of Fuller and designed by Eugene J. Mackey Jr. (see fig. 25); it was the first geodesic dome used as a greenhouse conservatory featuring different climatic zones.[3] In 1961 Fuller and his company, Synergetics Inc., designed the Union Tank Car Company Dome in Wood River, Illinois, housing the repair and maintenance of railroad cars.[4] This design replicated his design for the same company in Baton Rouge, Louisiana (1958; demolished 2008); these two domes were the world's largest clear-span structures at the time. The Mary Brown Center (1968), a community center in East St. Louis, was a built example of Fuller's 1965 Laminar Geodesic Dome patent, which made improvements with the fabrication of extremely lightweight domes utilizing laminar parts comprising thin inner- and outer-facing sheets.[5] The final realized design by Fuller for the St. Louis region was the Religious Center Dome (1971), in partnership with Shoji Sadao, at SIU's Edwardsville campus on the 90th meridian, which Fuller referred to as our planet's great circle main street, connecting two-thirds of all humanity.[6] It features a geo-scope—the only in existence: a 40-foot diameter, three-quarter sphere transparent miniature Earth.

Fuller's most dramatic, but unrealized, design, however, was Old Man River's City.[7]

72   Buckminster Fuller with a student-built geodesic dome at Washington University, St. Louis, 1955.

East St. Louis: A City in Decline

East St. Louis, founded in 1861 on the banks of the Mississippi River across from St. Louis, had grown to be the fourth largest city in Illinois by 1950, with a population of 82,366. This important railroad center, second in Illinois only to Chicago at the time, brought workers for nearby aluminum, steel, and chemical plants and stockyards. A gambling town with a red-light district, in the 1950s it underwent a "wave of reform [that] drove these activities out of sight, if not out of town."[8] In 1959 the National Civic League named East St. Louis an All-American City, but in the 1960s it began to have serious economic problems and an increase in crime and unemployment.[9]

According to the Federal Reserve Bank of St. Louis, "Between 1960 and 1970, the city lost nearly 70 percent of its businesses. Unemployment soared. Residents moved out of town. The population drain continued for years. Between 1970 and 2000, the city lost 55 percent of its population."[10] In 1960 African Americans made up 45 percent of the population of 82,000, compared to 98 percent in 2000 of the population of 30,000. The dramatic loss and relocation of jobs in the 1950s and 1960s resulted from restructuring in heavy industries, including railroads and meat-packing, to avoid paying high union labor costs and property taxes, according to Jennifer Hamer, the author of *Abandoned in the Heartland: Work, Family, and Living in East St. Louis*.[11] Increasing poverty and violence affected residential safety, downtown businesses, and the city's economic viability. The construction of the freeway system through East St. Louis further contributed to the city's decline, dividing functioning neighborhoods and social and community networks.

In 1964 Katherine Dunham returned to her home state of Illinois and joined the staff of SIU as an artist in residence, where she met Fuller. In 1967 she founded the Performing Arts Training Center in East St. Louis; in 1969 she and her husband, John Pratt, moved there; and in 1979 she opened the Dunham Dynamic Museum. Her dance company toured abroad from the 1930s through the 1950s—her international reputation helped draw dancers, artists, scholars, and musicians from around the world to the community, inspiring and educating both children and adults.[12]

On October 12, 1967, an Economic Opportunity Commission Hearing was held regarding the dire housing situation in East St. Louis. Both Dunham and Wyvetter H. Younge, a member of the Commission and a lifelong resident of East St. Louis, made statements at this hearing.[13] According to Younge, "The problem of low-cost housing in East St. Louis is that there is no low-cost housing in East St. Louis."[14] Dunham, speaking as both an internationally known figure and a concerned citizen of the region, cautioned, "When people live in hopelessness they become demoralized, and they become hardened if they are frustrated over and over."[15]

This eventually led Dunham to approach Fuller to design an urban housing development to address the city's housing problem.[16]

Old Man River's City: First Concept, 1970

On November 18, 1970, on the initiative of Dunham and with the support of the City Council of East St. Louis, Mayor Alvin G. Fields approved "A Resolution Establishing the East St. Louis Design and Development Team."[17] Fuller and his design team were to prepare an economic feasibility study for the development of the city's riverfront. They were instructed to "provide a forum in which all citizens and other interested parties can re-act to and make known their desires, wishes, and ideas for the development of the East St. Louis Riverfront."[18] Fuller declared, "[I will] develop the design and models at my own expense and do so without a fee." He went on to say, "what I would design must be so 'right' that the entire community would fall in love with it. . . or it would be dropped."[19]

73   Buckminster Fuller (center) with Washington University School of Architecture faculty and student design team, 1971.

To help with the design Fuller turned to his longtime friend, the architect James W. Fitzgibbon, professor of architecture and Fuller's partner in Synergetics Inc.[20] Fitzgibbon then organized a group of faculty and students in the School of Architecture at Washington University in St. Louis to assist (fig. 73).

74   Bill Wischmeyer with James W. Fitzgibbon,
model of Buckminster Fuller's Old Man River's City
(first concept), 1971.

The first design concept, *Old Man River, An Environmental Domed City: A Concept Design for E. St. Louis, IL* (1970–72), called for a city within a dome enclosure one-half mile in diameter (fig. 74). The dome's height was to be 900 feet, protecting 9,000 houses and apartments housing a population of 30,000 to 40,000. Community and commercial functions were to be located under the terraced housing structure, with parking for tenants and commercial users provided.[21] The dome's perimeter was to be elevated 30 feet above the site, open for ventilation and air movement through the dome's top, creating "a glazed, sun controlling, weather–temperature controlling umbrella." There were a limited number of access points into the domed city, connecting with surrounding highways and the proposed east side expansion of the Jefferson National Expansion Memorial along the East St. Louis riverfront. The project would have a density of approximately sixty families per acre.[22]

A pamphlet of the initial design concept was prepared with illustrations, drawings, site location, and written explanations by Fuller and Fitzgibbon:

Mr. Fuller determined on an approach which would recognize the necessity of a major project attempt to recover for East St. Louis a missing sense of community and civic pride and identity. This was to be an effort to make for East St. Louis a large scale civic-community venture which would be:
1. a comprehensive town, built within the city limits.
2. a project which would involve the best available environmental information and embody the best technological procedures directed toward a good life for all the people who would live in this town and in the area surrounding it.
3. a source of civic pride and identity, which in turn would tend to attract people, tourist interest, businesses, and capital investment in both the new town and in the region.
4. a demonstration that people could study, think about, and be involved in the design and accomplishment of a town and its promises of a decent living environment for its people.[23]

Old Man River's City: Town Hall Meeting, 1971

The design of Old Man River's City was first presented to the public at a town hall meeting on February 25, 1971, with two sets of five 4-foot by 8-foot display panels and a large-scale model prepared by the Washington University design team (figs. 75, 84).[24] Fuller presented his vision for a pollution-free city surrounded by parks, open land, boat marinas, and small lakes, extending southward toward the planned East Side Expansion.

75 Carl Safe, drawing of Buckminster Fuller's
Old Man River's City (first concept), 1971, photostat.

Within the half-mile diameter dome's interior, the "mountain" was to be made of four decks, each with ten concrete terraces of apartments, with views looking out to the parks, river, and sky (fig. 76). The apartments offered privacy with landscaped terraces. The center of the mountain accommodated shopping centers, recreation centers, schools, churches, motels, nightclubs, daycare centers, and other community-oriented services (fig. 77). Access to the dome would be via underground entranceways, allowing cars to enter. Modern transit systems

76 Christopher Grubbs, illustration of terraced housing inside Buckminster Fuller's Old Man River's City (first concept), 1971.

would take city dwellers to various locations within the dome. With a budget of approximately $500 million, Fuller said his plan got "the most for the least amount of money" and estimated a construction time of three years. He thought living there

77 Christopher Grubbs, illustration of interior of Buckminster Fuller's Old Man River's City (first concept), 1971.

would be within the economic reach of families on the lowest subsistence level above absolute poverty, with residents of East St. Louis given priority. Fuller emphasized his commitment to "do more with less" with this domed city, providing an enclosure with "the most volume with the least surface," resulting in operational efficiencies and a place that could be "a jumping off point for man to start enjoying the whole world."[25] He predicted this "unique," environment-controlled, domed city would focus world attention on East St. Louis, and in fact, in 1972 *The Architectural Forum* featured the Old Man River's City project in an issue titled "The World of Buckminster Fuller."[26] "I don't think there is anything I have ever done in my life before that could be so important," Fuller said.[27]

The approximately 130 people in attendance at the Mary Brown Center included a cross section of the East St. Louis community: local residents, a shopping center developer, a Chamber of

78   Buckminster Fuller is questioned by a member of the
East St. Louis community at the 1971 presentation of Old
Man River's City, as Wyvetter H. Younge, chairman of the
East St. Louis Plan Commission, listens.

Commerce manager, a city engineer, a Black Panther or two,
the War Lords leadership, a local high school newspaper editor,
a local pastor, and "the traditional political leaders." They
reacted "with stunned fascination, with cautious questioning
and with tentative approval" (figs. 78, 79).[28] One person in attendance said, "We don't need domes, we need jobs." Fuller
responded, "Young man, I see a future where you don't need
jobs." This exchange revealed a fundamental disconnection
between a citizen hoping for a better life and a visionary designer
with a utopian view. Another person expressed concern about
the limited number of entry points, saying it could become
"a glass-walled prison for blacks that could be sealed off in times
of racial tension, a place where even the air could be controlled
and someday it could be full of dead black people." Although
Fuller believed his plan would be "free of class distinctions" and
would create "a city that would celebrate the fact that there
is no race," the community responses led to dramatic design
revisions for the next version of Old Man River's City, with a
"dome umbrella" elevated 500 feet above the earth, protecting,
but not entrapping, the occupants of this new city.[29]

79   Buckminster Fuller, 120-foot diameter "model home" dome
for Old Man River's City (first concept, 1971), designed to be built
as a walk-in model to facilitate community feedback following
the town hall meeting.

Old Man River's City: Second Concept, 1973

Now titled *Old Man River–An Umbrellaed Town Concept for East St. Louis, Illinois* (1973), Fuller's second design was twice the diameter as the first, housing four times the population within the terraced "moon-crater" city, with inward facing communal spaces open to a dome whose bottom rim was sixteen times higher above the ground than that of the original design (fig. 80).[30]

The plan grew to accommodate 125,000 in a "moon-crater" city of 50 terraced stories and 500 feet in height, providing 25,000 landscaped, terraced garden homes, each with an outward view and 2,500 square feet of floor area. The inner surface of the crater was terraced for communal use, workspaces, and recreation area, with sporting venues located at the center, all under a one-mile-diameter geodesic, quarter-sphere, transparent umbrella mounted high above to permit full, all-around viewing below the umbrella's bottom perimeter. The top of the dome was to be 1,000 feet high, with the bottom of the dome's rim set at 500 feet above the terrain (figs. 81–83). With this change, the dome became a protective "umbrella," losing the "sun controlling, weather-temperature controlling dome" originally planned.

Approximately ten million square feet within the three-and-one-half-mile circumference terraced crater were to accommodate commercial space, factories, offices, parking lots, and services, including communal services not requiring daylight such as "all the multi-level trolley ways, interlevel ramps, roadways and parking lots with numerous radial crosswalks and local elevators." The crosswalks would allow residents to walk home from the interior community bowl to their private dwellings with views to the distant surroundings. Fuller proposed that each 2,500-square-feet apartment be 25 feet wide and 100 feet deep, extending into the mountainside. This would result in a 15-foot-deep, 25-foot-wide exterior terrace. Each of the 25,000 families would also have use of 1,300 square feet of public space on one of the 50 inward-facing communal terraces.[31]

The moon-crater and its terraces were to be constructed of thin-walled reinforced concrete supported by 500-foot-high, 2,000-foot-wide A-frame structural segments with 100 circumferential columns supporting trusses for the one-mile diameter, quarter-sphere dome covered with wire-reinforced glass

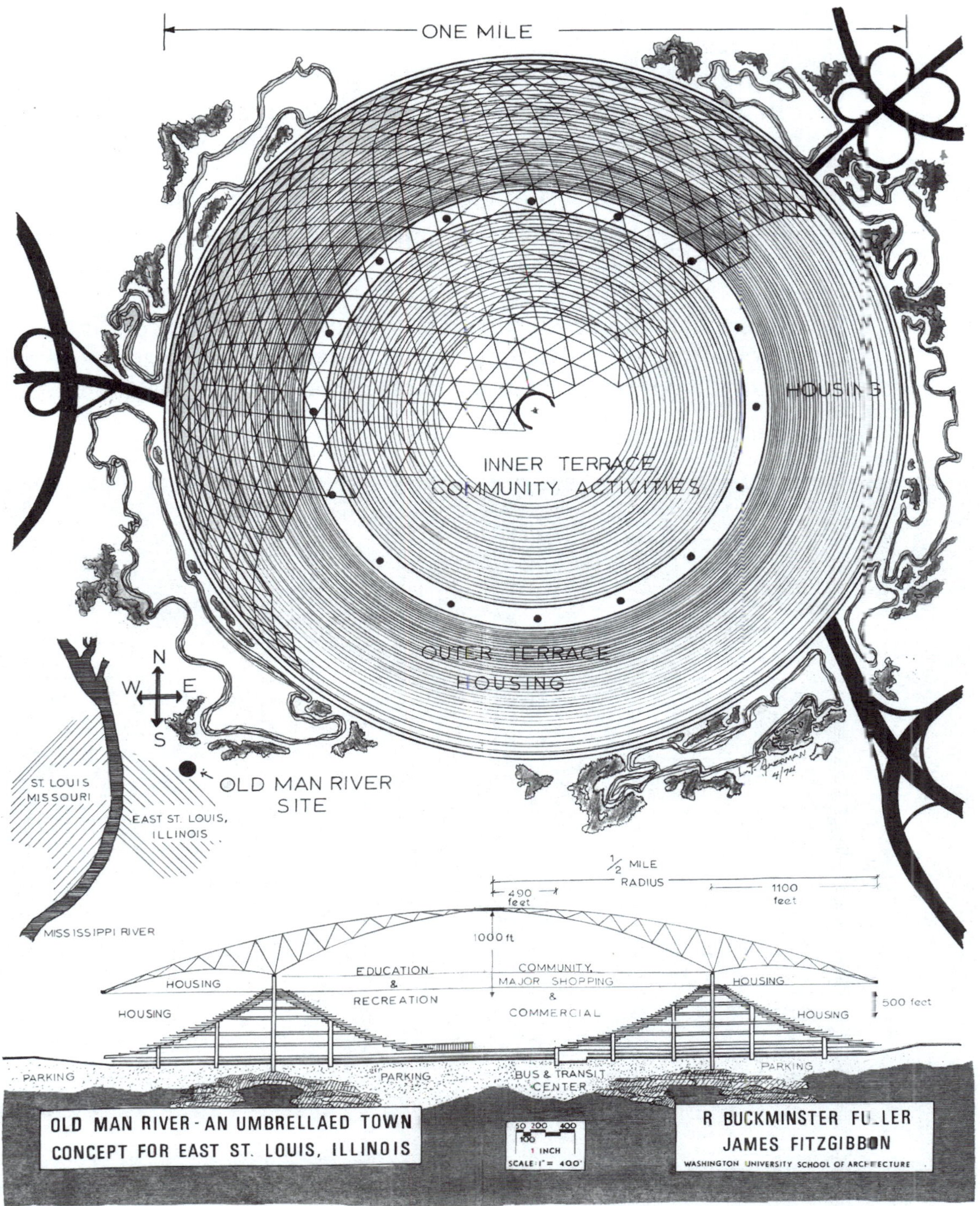

80 Buckminster Fuller and James W. Fitzgibbon
Old Man River's City (second concept), 1973.

admitting "life-supporting Sun radiation." Optimum construction efficiency would be achieved "with modern, high-speed highway-building equipment and earth-moving techniques as well as with suspension bridge-building and air-space technologies."[32] Fitzgibbon noted the vast quantities of materials to be used could lead to East St. Louis becoming revitalized as a manufacturing center, producing materials for the Old Man River's City project and other locations across the US, with similar new cities being constructed. Labor employment would enhance the economy of East St. Louis.[33]

Fuller calculated his proposed solution was 98 percent more efficient than a conventional design in terms of heat loss and gain, given the common walls and roofs of the 25,000 dwelling units.

81   Buckminster Fuller, Old Man River's City (second concept), 1973, elevation view of model.

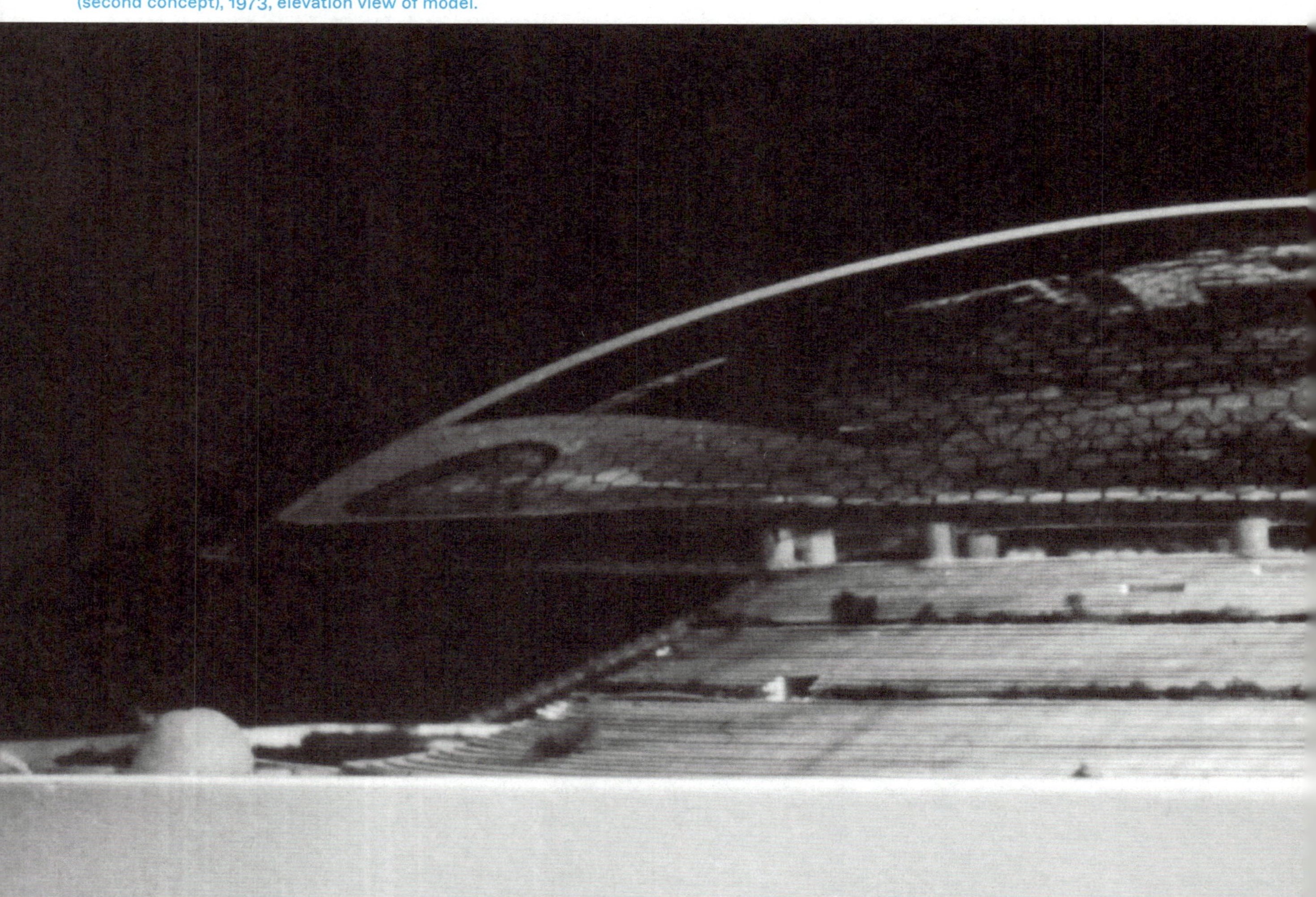

He believed Old Man River's City's environment would have a naturally mild climate, and that neither rain nor snow would drift inward ("no weather roofs") due to the "mass inertia of the vast quantity of atmosphere embraced by the umbrella as well as by the vertical mass of the crater's cone within the dome."[34] Structural efficiency, useful volume, and energy conservation were all optimized.

The dome watershed would collect rainfall runoff in a dome-level reservoir which in turn would supply the water needed for a high-pressure fire sprinkler and service purification systems, with surplus rainwater directed down to a "moat reservoir" surrounding the domed city–a feature that recalled the initial design with parks, open land, boat marinas, and small lakes surrounding the new city.[35]

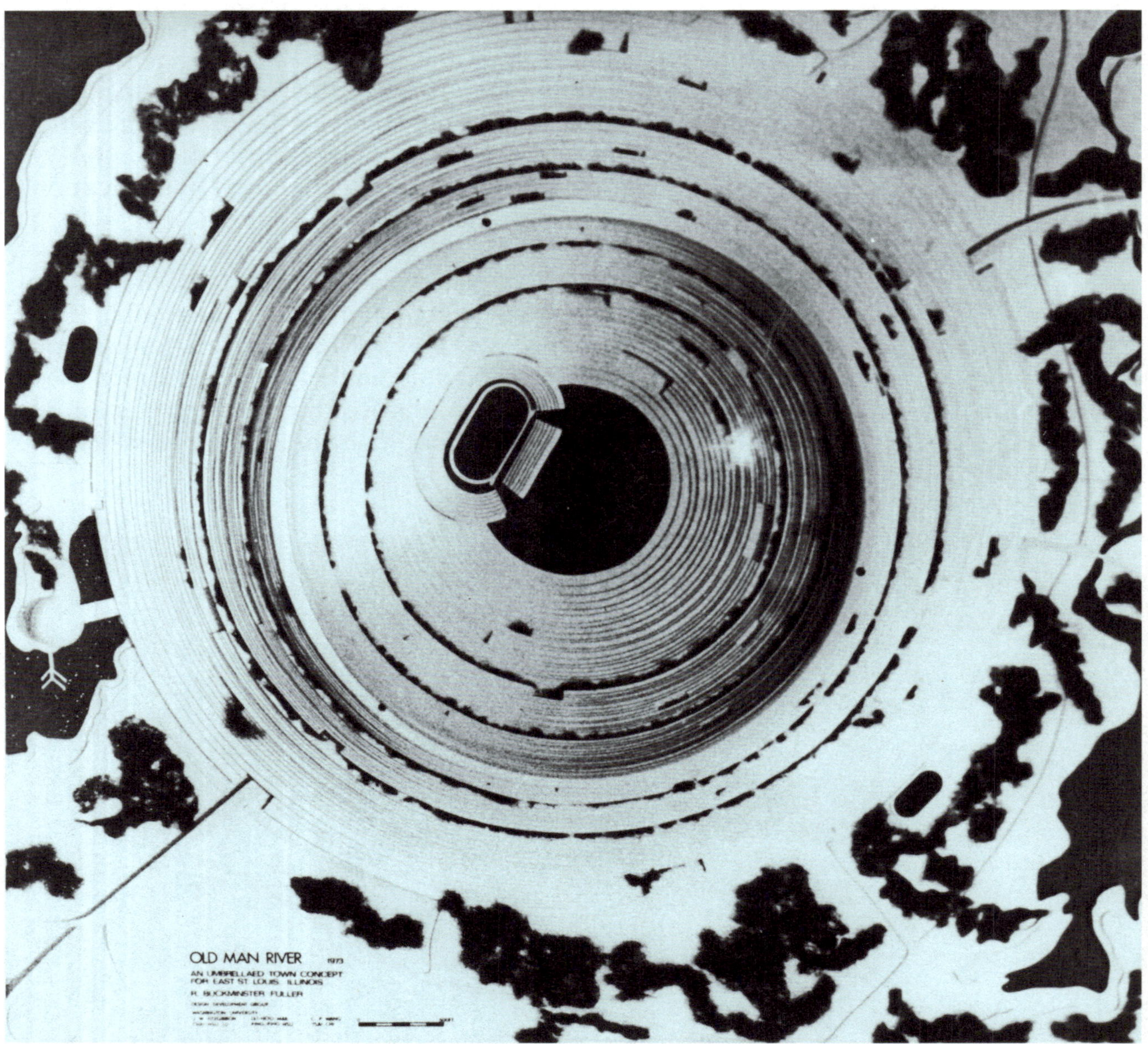

82   Buckminster Fuller, Old Man River's City
(second concept), 1973, plan view of model.

83   John C. Guenther, digital rendering of Buckminster
Fuller's Old Man River's City (second concept), superimposed
on a Google Earth aerial view of East St. Louis, 2020.

Financing and Realizing Old Man River's City

From the outset of the project, Fuller cautioned the citizens
and officials of East St. Louis to resolve "not to compromise our
design solution in order to qualify for any private foundation
or government subsidy funds," noting such funds would come
with restrictions and compromises that would adversely affect
the design rationale. Fuller advised East St. Louisans of the need
to develop the design, production, and assembly logistics strictly
according to individual and communal best interests, asserting
that economic support would materialize because this design
and approach was what humanity needed.[36] Fuller considered
it a success when he dissuaded the community from accepting
governmental funding. The economic support he predicted,
however, never came.

Nevertheless, Younge continued her commitment to the project.
After her election to the Illinois House of Representatives in 1974
she introduced a bill to help fund Old Man River's City, something she repeated every year, past Fuller's death in 1983, until
her own death in 2008.[37]

In 1995, participants in the "East St. Louis Syntegration on Old Man River's City" gathered to discuss strategies for how the project might be realized. The event was attended by Younge and organized by Harry Frederick William ("Bill") Perk, who studied under Fuller. Rowland and Dawn Brohawn, both members of the federal Center for Economic and Social Justice (CESJ)—an all-volunteer education center, grassroots think tank, and social action catalyst— introduced the concept of the for-profit, citizen-owned Community Investment Corporation. This led to the introduction of the first proposed legislation for establishing the Citizen Land Development Cooperatives by Younge in early 2004. Younge was resoundingly successful in getting the legislation through the Illinois House of Representatives by a vote of 114-0. However, after her death, without her leadership and dedication, the bill never went forward.[38]

Throughout his life Fuller remained optimistic that Old Man River's City would eventually be built, when the world was ready to accept it. With East St. Louis's urban decline still a pressing issue today (its population in 2022 had shrunk to 18,195), Old Man River's City remains unbuilt, leaving the African American–majority community still in need of better housing.

84 Buckminster Fuller in front of his domed city design at its first public showing at a town hall meeting in the Mary Brown Center, East St. Louis, Illinois, 1971.

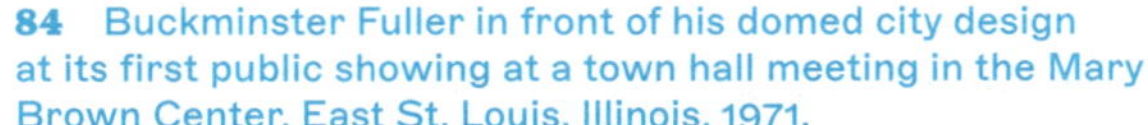

1   Alec Nevala-Lee, *Inventor of the Future: The Visionary Life of Buckminster Fuller* (New York: Dey St., 2022). Prominent among Fuller's international projects are the American National Exhibition Dome in Moscow (1959), the United States pavilion at the Montreal Expo 67, and the Triton Floating City Project for Tokyo (1960s).

2   Cary O'Dell and Thad Heckman, *Bucky's Dome: The Resurrection of R. Buckminster Fuller and Anne Hewlett Fuller's Dome Home in Carbondale, Illinois* (Arcadia Publishing, 2020), 20.

3   Eric Mumford, *Missouri Botanical Garden Climatron: A Celebration of 50 Years* (St. Louis: Missouri Botanical Garden, c. 2009), esp. 40, 48.

4   "Union Tank Car Company Dome," Society of Architectural Historians, SAH Archipedia (website), accessed March 27, 2024, https://sah-archipedia.org /buildings/IL-01-119-0090.

5   The patent was filed May 27, 1960, and granted August 31, 1965. See https:// ppubs.uspto.gov/dirsearch-public/print /downloadPdf/3203144.

6   See Lloyd Steven Sieden, *Buckminster Fuller's Universe* (New York: Basic Books, 1989), 264–65.

7   Fuller chose the name from the iconic song "Ol' Man River," popularized by Paul Robeson. The song "dramatized the life of Afro-American blacks who lived along the south-of-St. Louis banks of the Mississippi River in the days of heavy north-south river traffic in cotton," with lyrics sung from the perspective of enslaved African Americans. R. Buckminster Fuller, *Critical Path*, 1st ed. (New York: St. Martin's, 1981), 315.

8   John H. Allan, "East St. Louis: Decay and Deficit," *New York Times*, May 14, 1972, https://www.nytimes.com/1972/05/14 /archives/east-st-louis-urban-bankruptcy -business-flees-taxes-slide-us-rescue .html.

9   "East St. Louis: One City's Story," Federal Reserve Bank of St. Louis (website), December 31, 2002, https:// www.stlouisfed.org/publications /bridges/winter-20022003/east-st -louis-one-citys-story.

10 Ibid.

11 Jennifer Hamer, *Abandoned in the Heartland: Work, Family, and Living in East St. Louis* (Berkeley: University of California Press, 2011). See also Emily Banas's review of that book, "Book Corner: A Closer Look at East St. Louis, Ill., a City in Peril," University of Illinois, Urbana-Champaign, News Bureau, November 17, 2011, https://news.illinois .edu/view/6367/209544.

12 Joyce Aschenbrenner, *Katherine Dunham: Dancing a Life* (Urbana: University of Illinois Press, 2002); and "Katherine Dunham: Legacy," Missouri Historical Society (website), accessed March 31, 2024, https://mohistory.org/legacy -exhibits/KatherineDunham/legacy.htm.

13 Wyvetter H. Younge, later a state representative to the Illinois General Assembly, was an attorney—with a JD from Saint Louis University's School of Law and an LLM from Washington University's School of Law—and an assistant circuit attorney for the City of St. Louis.

14 "Wyvetter Younge Statement," Old Man River's City Revisited (website), version 2, updated May 7, 2020, https://iris.siue .edu/scalar/omr/media/ wyvetter-younge-statement-1.

15 "Katherine Dunham Statement," Old Man River's City Revisited (website), version 2, updated May 7, 2020, https:// iris.siue.edu/scalar/omr/media /katherine-dunham-statement-1.

16 Fuller, *Critical Path*, 315.

17 "A Resolution Establishing the East St. Louis Design and Development Team," in *The Notebooks: Old Man River Project*, an unpublished compilation of documents about the history and evolution of Old Man River's City, compiled by James W. Fitzgibbon, September 1972; courtesy of Carl Safe.

18 Fitzgibbon, *Notebooks*, 2.

19 Fuller, *Critical Path*, 322.

20 James W. Fitzgibbon, AIA, had been a professor of architecture at North Carolina State University (1948–1958), head of the Fuller Research Foundation, and Fuller's business partner in three companies: Skybreak Carolina Corporation; Geodesics Inc.; and Synergetics Inc. In 1968 Fitzgibbon took a leave of absence from Synergetics to teach as a visiting professor of architecture at Washington University in St. Louis.

21 R. Buckminster Fuller and James W. Fitzgibbon, *Old Man River, An Environmental Domed City: A Concept Design for E. St. Louis, IL*, pamphlet (Parsimonious Press, 1972), unpaged; courtesy of Carl Safe.

22 Fitzgibbon, *Notebooks*, 40–45.

23 Ibid., 40.

24 The design team included Washington University faculty members Thomas Thomson and Carl B. Safe, who produced a sectional drawing of the design concept, and students Christopher A. Grubbs (who produced renderings to illustrate the design concept), Jaturapat Israngkul, Marjorie Ann Miller (now Brownstein), Kathleen Page, Bill Wischmeyer (who produced an expansive scaled model of the proposed design showing its relationship to its site), and Gordon Wittenberg Jr. David Jordan, a photographer with Obata Studios in St. Louis, photographed the large-scale model of the project. As the design evolved, Dennis Cope, then an architecture graduate student in an independent studies program with Fitzgibbon, built models, provided cost estimates, and prepared Critical Path Method (CPM) diagrams to identify tasks necessary for the project completion and to determine project schedule, flexibilities, and flow. I thank Dennis Cope, Chris Grubbs, Carl Safe, Tom Thomson, and Bill Wischmeyer for our conversations from which this information derives.

25 Fuller, as quoted in John Shaffer, "Fuller's Vision: City under Dome," *Metro-East Journal*, February 26, 1971; courtesy of Carl Safe.

26 "The World of Buckminster Fuller," *The Architectural Forum* 136, no. 1 (January/ February 1972), 49–96, esp. 90, https:// dahp.wa.gov/sites/default/files /ArchitecturalForum-1972-Jan-Feb.pdf.

27 Fuller, as quoted in Shaffer, "Fuller's Vision."

28 Rube Yelvington, "Fuller's Dream for East St. Louis Everyone Has a Place under the Sun," *Metro-East Journal*, February 26, 1971; courtesy of Carl Safe.

29 Ibid., and conversations with Dennis Cope, Chris Grubbs, Carl Safe, Tom Thomson, and Bill Wischmeyer.

30 The design development group for this concept included James W. Fitzgibbon and students Chai-Hsu Lu, Lei-Hoo Mak, Ping-Ping Hsu, and C. P. Wang. They built a detailed massing model with a glass dome hovering above the terraces, set within the context of the site. I thank Tim Noakes, Head of Public Services, Department of Special Collections, Stanford University, for confirmation of the design team names (February 21, 2020).

31 Fuller, *Critical Path*, 316–17.

32 Ibid., 321.

33 Fitzgibbon, *Notebooks*, 35.

34 Fuller, *Critical Path*, 320–21.

35 Ibid., 316.

36 Ibid., 321–22.

37 Greg Bailey, "East St. Louis and the Old Man River Project," History and Headlines (website), March 14, 2018; updated April 27, 2020, https://www .historyandheadlines.com/east-st-louis -and-the-old-man-river-project/.

38 dawn, "1995 East St. Louis Syntegration on Old Man River City," September 29, 2015, https://www.uniteamericaparty.org /syntegration_esl_1995_page_2/.

A Modernist Memoir Made in St. Louis

Michael E. Willis, FAIA, NOMA

Modernist Stuttgart: Staatsgalerie and Weissenhofsiedlung

In 2016 I visited Stuttgart, Germany, to look at some icons of modernist architecture. I called my tour "Stuttgart: Modernism without Stress" because in my view modernism was an active influence in the architecture of Stuttgart, and at the time, there was a discussion about whether modernism as a movement was dead. I found the opposite: it was alive and evolving. My first stop was the Staatsgalerie Stuttgart, a postmodernist icon—James Stirling at his finest, with a little bit of Memphis thrown in (fig. 85). Unlike other postmodernist icons, it doesn't appear to have turned into a joke. A big concept, color, lots of internal light—and it still works as a museum, still works as a building. (I can't say the same for Michael Graves's Portland building, but I'll save that for another discussion.) My aim was to find the origin of modernist housing in the United States. I made it a mission to go to the source, the Weissenhofsiedlung—the 1927 complex of "workers' housing" consisting mostly of white boxes by Peter Behrens, Walter Gropius, Le Corbusier, Mies van der Rohe, J. J. P. Oud, Bruno Taut, and others—to see how that served as a benchmark for urban housing around the world, including St. Louis's Pruitt-Igoe housing project (1950–56, see fig. 40; demolished 1972–76). I'll get to that later. The Siedlung is still occupied and is a model of urban housing: close to services, walkable, and connected to transportation. It is not just a study for theoretical observation; it is to this day a workable, living community.

What impressed me about the architecture of Stuttgart is how it embraces classical modernism and creates a texture suited to its times, without nostalgia, without slavish imitation, but with a sense of openness and even fun. What it means to me is that such architecture can and should be about the energy of the city, interesting chapters written in different eras.

85   James Stirling and Michael Wilford & Associates, Neue Staatsgalerie, Stuttgart, Germany, 1979–84.

Modernist St. Louis: Pruitt-Igoe and LaClede Town

I was one of the first residents of Pruitt-Igoe. I moved in with my family—my mother, father, four sisters, and a younger brother—in 1956 at 2140 Cass Avenue. It was a new building and as close to the original ideals of the European modernists for mass housing as our segregated history would allow—a grouping of eleven-story buildings, rectangular and standing in whole blocks, "tabula rasa'd" and consolidated into a single field. From there I walked a block to Blewett School with my sisters, past the Crunden Branch Library (fig. 86)—itself a modernist design—carrying our money for milk in pyramidal containers. Sealtest milk, I think. We played with the other kids of all races on the open fields. Remember that sentence.

86   Joseph H. Senne, Frederick M. Crunden Branch Library,
serving Pruitt-Igoe, Vaughn, and Carr Square public housing
projects, St. Louis, 1959, photograph 1960.

87 Harris Armstrong and Hellmuth, Obata + Kassabaum (HOK),
Plaza Square, St Louis, 1957–61.

We left Pruitt-Igoe in 1959. In 1972, when it was blown up, it was deemed to be, to use Charles Jencks's term, "the death of modernism." Except that it wasn't. I point you to Hellmuth, Obata + Kassabaum's Plaza Square—nearly the same as Hellmuth, Yamasaki + Leinweber's design for Pruitt-Igoe but with additions brought by the brilliant Harris Armstrong: an emphasis on color, balconies, finishes, and being close to services and transportation (figs. 42, 87). Begun in 1957, it is still a desirable place to live.

By 1964 we had moved to LaClede Town (figs. 44, 88, 89). It was a magical place, a kind of urban Brigadoon. A cluster of houses, on a grid of streets, punctuated by circle roundabouts, play spaces, a grocery store, the Circle Coffeehouse, a laundromat, and the Coach and Four Pub, as well as a newspaper—*The Mill Creek Valley Intelligencer*. It was a small community, so small

that I was hired by Jerry Berger, the manager and curator
of LaClede Town, to create address boards with magic marker
on cardboard for the fifty or so residents until the aluminum
numbers arrived. Jerry made LaClede Town a place for artists
and writers, and it was multiracial at a time when that was a
new thing. The houses by Chloethiel Woodard Smith looked like
a neighborhood—not a set of blocks but a series of two- and
three-story structures in brick and wood siding. I learned later
that the builder, Isadore E. Millstone, would have liked to have
clad them all in brick for longevity, but the budget was not there.

88   Children playing in a courtyard in LaClede Town, late 1960s.

LaClede Town was where I first saw a man with a ponytail, Jerry
Faires. He managed the Circle Coffeehouse for a while, had
a twelve-string guitar strung with piano wire so he could play
sitar-inspired Indian ragas, and was in a psychedelic band called
the Crystalline Silence with jewelry-maker Ric Blackerby.
Ric painted black-and-white hypnotic Op Art spirals all over the
interior of his house, and his motorcycle-riding wife (Ria, I think)
was a nude model for my figure-drawing class some years later
when I was a student at Washington University. I worked in
the Circle Coffeehouse after school, heard Oliver Lake's Black
Artist Group (BAG) play free jazz, met a few famous jazz and

blues players (John Mixon on bass, Philip Williams on drums), saw my first Sartre play—*No Exit*, directed by local John Camie—and served espresso by the cupful. We went to Waring School, where Augustus C. Clark was the administrator, principal, and sole teacher. There were so few of us in LaClede Town that we were in a kind of one-room schoolhouse, housed in Harris Teachers College (now Harris-Stowe State University), but the school district sent us supplies for an entire school building: paper, volleyballs, jump ropes. We got to hear lectures from people like Michael Harrington (*The Other America*), who came to Harris to visit his mother. The streets were full of hipsters, college professors, radical reverends like Carl Dudley and Don Register of the adjacent Berea Presbyterian Church, and Santa in a Rolls Royce at Christmas (Jerry Berger). Imagination was on display for all. And by day we played with the other kids of all races on the open fields. Remember that sentence? LaClede Town was also demolished. The LaClede Town family, however, is still connected—the musicians, the people who grew up there—bonded by memory.

89 LaClede Town General Store, 1970.

Washington University; the University of California, Berkeley; and Charles E. Fleming

There's a photo from 1966 of members of the Urban Housing Foundation, a task force that advised inner-city communities on the development and preservation of housing (fig. 90). I know three of them: Jerry Berger; Roger Montgomery, director of the Urban Design Center at Washington University; and Charles E. Fleming, architect. Jerry I've already mentioned.

By a Post-Dispatch Photographer

Four of seven founders of the Urban Housing Foundation, Inc., at a board of directors meeting. They are (from left): Elisha Brown, Charles Fleming, Prof. Roger Montgomery and Jerome Berger.

90   Urban Housing Foundation directors pictured in an article in the *St. Louis Post-Dispatch*, 1966.

In 1969 I enrolled in the School of Architecture at Washington University. I was ready for the new world (except for the occasional bout of imposter syndrome). My classmates were brilliant, my teachers encouraged me, and we built many models and put on many exhibits, on campus and beyond. Our courses were not just confined to the academic classroom—we were involved in bringing architecture to St. Louis. We participated in city street fairs; we sold art on the streets. As part of our education about St. Louis architecture, my fellow classmate Jim Stokoe and I were asked to build a model re-creating the office of the late modernist icon Harris Armstrong in one of the design studios in Givens Hall, Washington University's architecture building. We staged it in detail, down to his cigar cutter. It meant visiting Armstrong's wife at their home, where his office was, which was also an opportunity to see his Airstream trailer that he converted into an adjunct office for partners he brought onto his projects.

Immediately after graduation in 1976 I worked for SRT (Spector Royse & Trivers) Architects, and then later I went to work for Charles Fleming and the Jenkins-Fleming firm. My story on how I got there is that I walked past Charles's Neighborhood Health Center at the intersection of Easton Avenue (now Martin Luther King Jr. Drive) and Belt Avenue (see fig. 26). I looked at the building and told myself that I wanted to work for whoever designed it. I had no idea it was Charles's firm. I went to the office, applied, and worked there from 1976 to 1980. I designed many parks for Jenkins-Fleming, including Bellerive, Penrose, Fairground, and Fountain Parks. In 1979 I was invited by Mary Comerio, a former Washington University classmate who after graduation went to the University of California, Berkeley, to come and teach for a semester in 1980. That's where I met Roger Montgomery, who became an acquaintance; we continued to meet for coffee years after he retired. I also met my future bride who, in a rare happenstance, was being admitted to the UC Berkeley School of Social Welfare. Then back to St. Louis to work for Eugene Mackey in the Railway Exchange building until 1982, when I moved to San Francisco to work in the city of my fiancée. Prior to the move, at a chance meeting in St. Louis with Charles, I told him of my California plans. He offered me the opportunity to open the San Francisco office of the Fleming Corporation, which I accepted. We specialized in public works and public housing. Our first new housing project was fifty-one new units for the low-income affordable senior retirement complex Allen Temple Arms II in Oakland. By the time I left in 1988 the office had fourteen people employed. I then opened my own firm, Michael Willis & Associates Architects. I retired from MWA Architects in 2016.

91 Percy Green II and Richard Daly, members of CORE (Congress of Racial Equality), climb the Jefferson National Expansion Memorial (Gateway Arch) to protest the exclusion of Black construction workers from the project as an official attempts to persuade them to come down, 1964.

Modernist St. Louis: What Remains

Many modernist icons in St. Louis still remain: Council Plaza with its Richard Henmi–designed "saucer" (see fig. 43); homes by William Adair Bernoudy (see figs. 20, 21) and Edouard Jules Mutrux; Gyo Obata's Lambert–St. Louis Airport terminal with its fluid shapes in concrete (see figs. 38, 48, 49); Fleming's Neighborhood Health Clinic (see fig. 26); the endangered but still-with-us J. C. Penney building by William McMahon in nearby Wellston; the Buckminster Fuller–inspired Climatron for the Missouri Botanical Garden (see fig. 25); Eero Saarinen's Gateway Arch (figs. 3, 91, 92).

We can still be inspired by what we see, and by the vision of a new world, made of concrete, glass, and steel geometries, less dependent on the ornament and strictures of the past than on the open thoughts and imaginations of the city's new inhabitants: modern people, living in modern times and modern spaces, taking a fresh look at how cities are made.

92 Michael Van Valkenburgh Associates, renovations to Dan Kiley's grounds of the Jefferson National Expansion Memorial (Gateway Arch), 2018.

Index

Image Credits

All reasonable efforts have been made to obtain permission for images reproduced in this volume. Please address any oversight to the publisher.

An American City: Four Years' Progress; St. Louis, 1949–1953 (St. Louis, 1953), University Libraries, Washington University in St. Louis, fig. 41; *Architectural Record* 102, no. 3 (September 1947): 102, fig. 11; Harris Armstrong Collection, Julian Edison Department of Special Collections, Washington University Libraries, figs. 4, 9, 10; Arteaga Photos LTD, fig. 43; Photo by Richard G. Askew, courtesy of Cranbrook Archives, Cranbrook Center for Collections and Research, fig. 12; Photo by Lee Bey, figs. 66, 68; Photo by Shantel Blakely, figs. 57, 62; Courtesy of Kyrle Boldt, fig. 18; Courtesy of COCA - Center of Creative Arts, St. Louis, fig. 32; Courtesy of Congregation B'nai Amoona, St. Louis, figs. 27, 31; Courtesy of Dennis Cope, figs. 79, 81, 82; Courtesy of Cranbrook Academy of Art, https://openscholarship.wustl.edu/books/55, fig. 45; Photo by Arthur Fillmore, *Architectural Record* (Mid-May 1959): 112, fig. 50; Charles Fleming Collection, Missouri Historical Society, St. Louis, figs. 26, 58, 59, 60, 61, 65; Courtesy of the Fleming family, fig. 63; Gateway Arch National Park Archives, fig. 2; Gottscho-Schleisner Collection, Prints and Photographs Division, Library of Congress, Washington, DC, fig. 48; Courtesy of Christopher Grubbs and Dennis Cope, figs. 76, 77; Courtesy of John C. Guenther, figs. 73, 78, 80, 83; Photo by David Gulick, *St. Louis Post-Dispatch* / Polaris, collection of Emily Rauh Pulitzer, figs. 20 (Estate of Jacques Lipchitz), 21; HB-007051-B, Hedrich-Blessing Collection, Chicago History Museum, © Chicago Historical Society, fig. 7; HB-11317-O2, Hedrich-Blessing Collection, Chicago History Museum, © Chicago Historical Society, fig. 6; HB-19234-P, Hedrich-Blessing Collection, Chicago History Museum, © Chicago Historical Society, fig. 38; HB-23883, Hedrich-Blessing Collection, Chicago History Museum, © Chicago Historical Society, fig. 25; Photo by Hedrich-Blessing, *Architectural Forum* 89, no. 4 (October 1948): 74, Harris Armstrong Collection, Julian Edison Department of Special Collections, Washington University Libraries, © 2024 The Isamu Noguchi Foundation and Garden Museum, New York / Artists Rights Society (ARS), New York, fig. 5; Photo by Hedrich-Blessing, collection of the St. Louis Mercantile Library at the University of Missouri-St. Louis, figs. 13, 15; Courtesy of HOK, figs. 46, 54, 56; Photo by David Jordan, courtesy of Carl Safe, fig. 74; Photo by Balthazar Korab, Balthazar Korab Collection, Prints and Photographs Division, Library of Congress, Washington, DC, fig. 51; Kunstbibliothek, Staatliche Museen zu Berlin, EM11c55, fig. 30; Kunstbibliothek, Staatliche Museen zu Berlin, EM11c70, fig. 33; Kunstbibliothek, Staatliche Museen zu Berlin, HdzEM990, fig. 29; Photo by Daniel T. Magidson, courtesy of the Saint Louis University Archives, fig. 89; Missouri Historical Society, St. Louis, fig. 88; Photo by Henry T. Mizuki, Missouri Historical Society, St. Louis, fig. 14; Photo by Eric P. Mumford, figs. 19, 22, 23, 42, 69, 70, 71, 92; Photo by Winifred Elysse Newman, fig. 52; Photo by Paul Ockrassa, *St. Louis Globe-Democrat*, courtesy of the St. Louis Mercantile Library, University of Missouri-St. Louis, fig. 64; Photo by Andrew Pielage, the Frank Lloyd Wright House, Ebsworth Park, fig. 16; Private collection, fig. 8; Photo by Ramon Royer, courtesy of the Saint Louis Abbey, fig. 53; Courtesy of Carl Safe, fig. 75; Courtesy of the Saint Louis Science Center, fig. 55; Courtesy of the Saint Louis University Archives, fig. 36; Photo by Jaime Silva, Creative Commons Attribution-Share Alike 4.0 International license, fig. 85; Photo by Lloyd Spainhower, courtesy of the Saint Louis Abbey, fig. 39; *St. Louis Globe-Democrat*, courtesy of the St. Louis Mercantile Library, University of Missouri-St. Louis, figs. 44, 87; *St. Louis Post-Dispatch* / Polaris, figs. 1, 28, 72, 90, 91; Photo by Ezra Stoller / Esto Photographics Inc., fig. 49; United States Geological Survey via Wikimedia Commons, fig. 40; University Libraries, Washington University in St. Louis, figs. 34, 35, 37; University Photographic Services Collection, University Archives, Washington University Libraries, fig. 24; Photo by T. V. Vessell, *St. Louis Globe-Democrat*, courtesy of the St. Louis Mercantile Library, University of Missouri–St. Louis, fig. 67; Photo by Leigh Weiner, courtesy of the Computer History Museum, Mountain View, CA, fig. 47; Photo by Arthur Witman, Arthur Witman Photograph Collection, State Historical Society of Missouri, figs. 3, 86; The Frank Lloyd Wright Foundation Archives (The Museum of Modern Art / Avery Architectural & Fine Arts Library, Columbia University, New York), fig. 17; Photo by Steve Yelvington, Creative Commons Attribution-Share Alike 4.0 International license, fig. 84.